Love, Subjectivity, and Truth

Love, Subjectivity, and Truth

Existential Themes in Proust

RICK ANTHONY FURTAK

OXFORD
UNIVERSITY PRESS

Oxford University Press is a department of the University of Oxford. It furthers the University's objective of excellence in research, scholarship, and education by publishing worldwide. Oxford is a registered trade mark of Oxford University Press in the UK and certain other countries.

Published in the United States of America by Oxford University Press
198 Madison Avenue, New York, NY 10016, United States of America.

© Oxford University Press 2023

All rights reserved. No part of this publication may be reproduced, stored in a retrieval system, or transmitted, in any form or by any means, without the prior permission in writing of Oxford University Press, or as expressly permitted by law, by license, or under terms agreed with the appropriate reproduction rights organization. Inquiries concerning reproduction outside the scope of the above should be sent to the Rights Department, Oxford University Press, at the address above.

You must not circulate this work in any other form
and you must impose this same condition on any acquirer.

Library of Congress Control Number: 2023934097

ISBN 978-0-19-763372-4

DOI: 10.1093/oso/9780197633724.001.0001

Printed by Integrated Books International, United States of America

to Ruth
"with feathers"

Contents

Preface ix
Acknowledgments xv

1. Love and the Meaning of Life   1
2. On Possibility and Significance   24
3. Skepticism and Perspective: The Elusiveness of Truth   39
4. On Loving Badly and Discovering Truth Nonetheless   116
5. "Reality as We Have Felt It to Be"   124

Index   145

Preface

i.

"*La vérité subjective*,"[1] a phrase used in Proust's novel, is rich with existential connotations. It invokes Kierkegaard above all, but significantly Nietzsche as well, and other philosophers whom we could name because they also thematize love, subjectivity, and truth. While there may be motives for defining the term existential*ism* so narrowly that it applies to two or three French authors only,[2] in classifying as "existential" the themes of this book I am speaking more broadly about what might be called existential philosophy or existential thought. I assume that the presence of a topic in Kierkegaard's corpus is enough reason to classify it as part of the "existential" tradition construed in this wide sense. And I have written elsewhere about Kierkegaard's work on love and subjectivity in relation to truth.[3] Furthermore, I believe that "what it means to understand one's own life as a work in progress" is a central issue for both fiction and existential thought,[4] and would add only that Proust's narrative is eminently an attempt to articulate

---

[1] Marcel Proust, *À la recherche du temps perdu*, ed. Jean-Yves Tadié et al., 4 volumes (Paris: Gallimard, 1987); I have consulted this edition throughout.

[2] As, e.g., Jonathan Webber does in *Rethinking Existentialism* (Oxford: Oxford University Press, 2018), 14–19.

[3] On subjectivity and truth, see Rick Anthony Furtak, "The Heart of Knowledge: Kierkegaard on Passion and Understanding," in *Kierkegaard's God and the Good Life*, ed. Stephen Minister, J. Aaron Simmons, and Michael Strawser (Bloomington: Indiana University Press, 2017), 114–129. On love and truth, see also Furtak, "Love as a Relation to Truth," *Kierkegaard Studies Yearbook* 18 (2013): 129–149.

[4] Yi-Ping Ong, *The Art of Being: Poetics of the Novel and Existentialist Philosophy* (Cambridge, MA: Harvard University Press, 2018), 195. "There must come a moment," Kierkegaard contends in *From the Papers of One Still Living*, when "life is

the quest for this kind of self-understanding in one's own life as it unfolds over time. His narrator is constantly engaged in the effort to understand himself in the midst of existence.

Insofar as it includes the conveyance and analysis of experience, the novel is capable not only of exploring existential issues but also of doing something like phenomenology. Kundera, who points out that "all the great existential themes" examined for instance by Heidegger are "unveiled, displayed, illuminated" in literary fiction, remarks as well that we find "superb 'phenomenological descriptions' in Proust."[5] His multi-volume novel is especially interested in the intermittencies of the heart, in what we come to know about others through love—and in our affective experience generally, from emotions such as jealousy to emotional dispositions such as anxious expectancy. "The search for lost time," as Ricoeur has written, deals in particular with love and coincides "with the search for truth,"[6] most notably the truth about love and subjectivity. That is why Proust's narrative dwells so much on *impressions*, and according to Kristeva also "blurs the boundaries of the felt and the thought,"[7] in addition to blurring the boundary between reporting about, and reflecting upon, experience.[8]

For this reason, *In Search of Lost Time* is often considered to be *the* novel of ideas par excellence.[9] That name is well merited for its

---

understood backward." See Søren Kierkegaard, *Early Polemical Writings*, trans. Julia Watkin (Princeton, NJ: Princeton University Press, 1990), 78. This is an unmistakably Proustian sentiment, as it were.

[5] Milan Kundera, *The Art of the Novel*, trans. Linda Asher (New York: Harper Perennial, 2000), 5 and 32.

[6] Paul Ricoeur, *Time and Narrative, Volume Two*, trans. Kathleen McLaughlin and David Pellauer (Chicago: University of Chicago Press, 1985), 139–140.

[7] Julia Kristeva, *Proust and the Sense of Time*, trans. Stephen Bann (New York: Columbia University Press, 1993), 80–82.

[8] As we shall see, the tension between reports and reflections is frequently significant.

[9] See, e.g., Morris Weitz, *Philosophy in Literature* (Detroit, MI: Wayne State University Press, 1963), 78 and 87; Duncan Large, "Proust on Nietzsche," *Modern Language Review* 88 (1993): 612–624, 613–614. See also Joshua Landy, *The World According to Proust* (Oxford: Oxford University Press, 2023).

detailed evocations of things that are concretely perceived, no less than for its theoretical speculations about the human condition. My approach is guided by the belief that what Proust's narrator tries to understand philosophically arises from his life,[10] and is inseparably bound up with it. To recount that life story, he meanders through first-person memories of what he has experienced and contemplates the meaning of it all. I will claim that Proust's work has something to teach us about the topics of love, subjectivity, and truth, if we as readers are willing to immerse ourselves completely in the texture of his incomparable prose narrative. And my intent is for *this* book to be not merely compatible, but continuous, with my (other) written work about emotion, literature, and existential thought.

ii.

What we know is shaped by our way of knowing, as the properties of visible, colored objects are determined by the wavelengths of light our eyes can see. Nowhere does the subjective basis of our awareness appear so evident as it does when we view things through loving eyes. In what he portrays as a Buddhist moment, Nietzsche goes so far as to assert that "love is the state in which man [sic] sees things most widely different from what they are. The force of illusion reaches its zenith here."[11] In Proust's novel we find similar declarations made time and time again. However, we also observe countercurrents repeatedly arising, in which love and related emotions are both shown and said to provide a unique type of

---

[10] The narrator's life, that is, which is not identical with that of Proust. On how we can be moved by the lives of fictional characters, see Ted Cohen, *Thinking of Others* (Princeton, NJ: Princeton University Press, 2008), 36–37.

[11] Friedrich Nietzsche, *The Antichrist*, trans. Anthony Ludovici (Amherst, NY: Prometheus Books, 2000), § 23. In the same section, he praises Buddhism for being "a hundred times colder, more truthful, more objective" than the religion of love, Christianity. Yet this is not Nietzsche's final word.

insight. At these times, love seems to be a prerequisite of veridical apprehension.

So, which is it? What I hope to offer is an investigation of this question as it is played out in its various permutations throughout *In Search of Lost Time*. After the next two chapters introduce our major themes and ease us into the contours of the Proustian universe, my third and longest chapter delves into the reasons given by Proust's narrator for being skeptical about what love is capable of revealing, alongside the opposed reasons for overcoming this skepticism. After arguing for how the latter could be viewed as carrying greater weight, I conclude by considering why it is that even a flawed subjectivity can have a big role in acquainting us with particular truths about human existence; then, I clarify the concept of love-based personal identity that Proust's novel ultimately endorses, an ideal of "real life" and "felt truth" that we can affirm through the courage of our emotions. The affective constitution of the world may, therefore, legitimately be viewed through something other than a skeptical eye.

This reading of Proust must reckon with the numerous motivations for skepticism about love that are rehearsed throughout *In Search of Lost Time*. As I categorize and evaluate these motives, I am attentive at once to the inference that, "if there is but one true world, there can be but one vision of truth," implying that a finite standpoint is untrustworthy,[12] and to the narrator's habit of denying the antecedent and embracing a plurality of truthful perspectives. From this side, what qualifies as objectively real for us is related to our affective vantage point,[13] delimited by our interests, passions, and concerns.

---

[12] Mary Rawlinson, "Art and Truth: Reading Proust," *Philosophy and Literature* 6 (1982): 1–16, 1. On Proust's status as a philosopher, see Franck Robert, *L'Écriture sensible: Proust et Merleau-Ponty* (Paris: Classiques Garnier, 2021), 21–28.

[13] See, e.g., Peter Poellner, "Perspectival Truth," in *Nietzsche*, ed. John Richardson and Brian Leiter (New York: Oxford University Press, 2001), 85–117, 98–99.

Readers who care about love and the meaning of life are invited to enter the pages that follow. Those who are not—yet—admirers of Proust are every bit as welcome as those who already are. This book is aimed first and foremost at a literary and philosophical audience, most of all at everyone who is in some way invested in both philosophy and literature. Furthermore, I hope this book will reach researchers into the psychology of emotions, in particular those readers who can appreciate why it is that "a person's interpretations of feelings and events are as fundamental to psychology as genes are to biology,"[14] and how one author's writing can clarify human existence for others. Into their hands I commend the spirit of this inquiry.

---

[14] Jerome Kagan, *Psychology's Ghosts: The Crisis in the Profession and the Way Back* (New Haven, CT: Yale University Press, 2012), 248. On the same page, he observes that "the neuroscientist's concept of fear ... does not capture the meaning" of, for example, a person's "fear that he had wasted his life." Regarding the pertinence of literature to psychology as a human science, see also Keith Oatley, *Best Laid Schemes: The Psychology of Emotions* (Cambridge: Cambridge University Press, 1992), 122–126.

Acknowledgments

I wrote most of these pages during the global health crisis that brought with it a lot of involuntary solitude for me, as for so many people. On the day that I finished the last revisions of the book, I heard someone claim that "the age of inwardness," represented by Rilke and presumably by Proust, among others, has decisively passed. This sounds like it might be a "merely academic" diagnosis, yet I share the feeling that something precious is currently threatened, something that literary philosophy seeks to protect. I have tried to do so.

My own solitude has been safeguarded and nourished during this time by Ruth Rebecca Tietjen, to whom I am most grateful. My longtime friendship and conversation with James D. Reid, Sharon Krishek, J. P. Rosensweig, and Alyssa Luboff, as well as Helen Daly, has had a strong and beneficial influence throughout this period on my life and work, too; all of them have provided vital assurances, along with perceptive reactions to my ideas. When I try to say what these friends mean to me, I find myself running into the unsayable.

I thank Eleanor Helms for organizing an APA session (online, of course) in which Troy Jollimore, Robbie Kubala, and Joshua Landy were involved. Their support and encouragement were invaluable, and both Troy and Josh continued to read and comment on further chapters in ways that fostered this book as it came into being. To a more modest extent, I am indebted to two anonymous readers along the way.

Particularly inspiring were the discussions during a seminar at the University of Pardubice's Centre for Ethics at which I presented, and I learned much from those who responded to parts of this text at the University of Copenhagen's Søren Kierkegaard Research Centre and in a conference session of the European Philosophical Society for the Study of Emotions. Several of them are named here below.

In addition to those mentioned above, insightful feedback was given to me also by Megan Altman, Laura Candiotto, Ulrika Carlsson, Lyra Koli, Jean Moritz Müller, Martha C. Nussbaum, Lucy Osler, Kamila Pacovská, Erin Plunkett, Iain D. Thomson, Íngrid Vendrell Ferran, and Imke von Maur. I am thankful to each of them for talking philosophy with me—as I am also to Nicole Hassoun, David L. Hildebrand, Marion Hourdequin, Boram Jeong, Frances Maughan-Brown, Willow Mindich, Sarah Pessin, Ella C. Street, and Maddy Wadolowski. Of all the students who have taught *me* and to whom I am beholden, I must single out Maria A. Keller, whose recital of Marcel's rhapsodic tribute to *jeunes filles* is forever inscribed in my memory. "Goodbye" is too good a word.

My family has been an utterly essential source of sustenance and comfort, as loving as ever, and I am always aware that I would not be here without them. My Colorado College colleagues have been supportive, too. Yet the only human being with whom I have been in touch every day is Ruth, without whose immeasurable care I could not have written any of this. She knows better than anyone else about the limits of language, and what can fit within them. It is to her that I dedicate this book—full-heartedly, and overflowing with gratitude.

1
Love and the Meaning of Life

i.

As we are reminded by the title of a well-known poem,[1] love calls us to the things of this world. Turning to existential phenomenology, we find this point being made in similar terms. It is, as Max Scheler explains, the "movement of my heart" as a loving or caring being that establishes my "many-sided interest in the things of this world."[2] The realm of "things which count and exist for me," in other words (those of Merleau-Ponty),[3] is defined by my ability to love. Our life in the world is experienced as meaningful *because* we are fundamentally loving beings: this affective capacity determines what has reality and value, as far as each of us is concerned. That is why, if we understand how love reveals the significance of things to us, "we shall thereby come to understand better how things and beings can exist in general."[4] In another book, I develop the concept of the emotional a priori—love, care, and concern—as what grounds our entire affective life, giving rise to a valuable world by opening our eyes to the meaning of what exists.[5] Love therefore

---

[1] Richard Wilbur, "Love Calls Us to the Things of This World," in *New and Collected Poems* (San Diego, CA: Harcourt Brace Jovanovich, 1988), 233–234.

[2] Max Scheler, "Ordo Amoris," in *Selected Philosophical Essays*, trans. David Lachterman (Evanston, IL: Northwestern University Press, 1973), 98–135, 98.

[3] Maurice Merleau-Ponty, *Phenomenology of Perception*, trans. Colin Smith (New York: Routledge, 2002), 333.

[4] Merleau-Ponty, *Phenomenology of Perception*, 178.

[5] Rick Anthony Furtak, *Knowing Emotions: Truthfulness and Recognition in Affective Experience* (New York: Oxford University Press, 2018), 103–121.

serves as "the foundation for every sort of knowing,"[6] just as the sun illuminates visible objects for those of us with eyes to see. If a person had never known love's influence, he or she would be like a blind person in relation to colors.[7] Through this mode of vision, we appreciate much that we would otherwise overlook.

It is by virtue of our underlying affective dispositions of love and care, which constitute the emotional a priori, that things matter from our vantage point, and are not perceived as being value-neutral. Here is Proust's narrator, depicting the home of his beloved Gilberte:

> My imagination had isolated and hallowed in social Paris a certain family, just as it had set apart in structural Paris a certain house, whose entrance it had sculpted and its windows bejewelled. But these ornaments I alone had eyes to see.... For in order to distinguish in everything that surrounded Gilberte an indefinable quality analogous in the world of the emotions to what in the world of colors is called infra-red, my parents would have needed that supplementary sense with which love had temporarily endowed me.[8]

Already, then, we have encountered an enigma. When he explains how this aspect of the world appears to him, he is not merely providing a descriptive account of the facts. In speaking about *the*

---

[6] Max Scheler, *The Constitution of the Human Being*, trans. John Cutting (Milwaukee: Marquette University Press, 2008), 391–392: love, he adds, allows for "the showing of something" to us, by revealing it in its significance.

[7] This metaphor is independently developed by Kierkegaard and by Scheler: see Søren Kierkegaard, *Christian Discourses*, trans. Howard V. Hong and Edna H. Hong (Princeton, NJ: Princeton University Press, 1997), 237; Max Scheler, *Formalism in Ethics and Non-Formal Ethics of Values*, trans. Manfred S. Frings and Roger L. Funk (Evanston, IL: Northwestern University Press, 1973), 255. Cf. Scheler, "Ordo Amoris," 117.

[8] *Swann's Way*, in *Remembrance of Things Past*, trans. C. K. Scott Moncrieff, Terence Kilmartin, and (for *Time Regained* only) Andreas Mayor, 3 volumes (New York: Vintage Books, 1982), I: 450. All citations of *À la recherche du temps perdu*, better rendered in English as *In Search of Lost Time*, will provide one of seven book titles, with page references to this translation and three-volume edition, unless otherwise indicated.

significance of things, he is noting a feature of his environment that depends upon his own subjective outlook in a way that other qualities of the world arguably do not.[9] So is Marcel (as I will refer to Proust's narrator)[10] detecting something actual that love enables him to discern, or is he endowing Gilberte's house with false properties through his infra-red vision? This question will perplex him throughout the novel, and in *this* book we will be contemplating it continuously as well, following his fluctuating theoretical views with a critical eye.

Infra-red vision, after all, does not spawn a fabricated world out of itself; rather, it brings to light something "out there" which is real yet invisible to most subjects. No logic determines what in our perceptual field ought to stand out and command our attention, and without the dispositional affects of love, care, concern, or interest—the emotional a priori, in my terminology—nothing in the world around us would be more salient than anything else.[11] Indeed, in this case we would be faced with a flat, disorganized mass of information, without a sense that any of it *matters* to us. For

---

[9] Robert C. Solomon observes that such qualities "are *in the world*, not in the subject's head or mind," but are "subject-dependent" nonetheless; confusedly, on the very same page he endorses the theoretical position that, "in love, we bestow charms and virtues on the beloved." *True to Our Feelings: What Our Emotions Are Really Telling Us* (Oxford: Oxford University Press, 2007), 55.

[10] See Proust, *The Captive*, III: 69. Of Albertine, his narrator says: "Then she would find her tongue and say: 'My --' or 'My darling --' followed by my Christian name, which, if we give the narrator the same name as the author of this book, would be 'My Marcel,' or 'My darling Marcel.'" I accept Marcel's invitation, but without intending to identify the author with his narrator. Joshua Landy comments upon how remarkable it is that the narrator knows what his creator is named: *Philosophy as Fiction: Self, Deception, and Knowledge in Proust* (New York: Oxford University Press, 2004), 22–23.

[11] On why no logic identifies that to which we ought to attend, see Ronald de Sousa, "The Rationality of Emotions," in *Explaining Emotions*, ed. Amélie O. Rorty (Berkeley & Los Angeles: University of California Press, 1980), 127–151, 136. See also Michael Stocker, "Some Considerations about Intellectual Desire and Emotions," in *Thinking about Feeling: Contemporary Philosophers on Emotions*, ed. Robert C. Solomon (New York: Oxford University Press, 2004), 135–148, 139: "Kierkegaard and Heidegger hold that without care, concern, and interest, nothing would be salient." Relatedly, see Matthew Ratcliffe, "The Phenomenology of Mood and the Meaning of Life," in *The Oxford Handbook of Philosophy of Emotion*, ed. Peter Goldie (Oxford: Oxford University Press, 2010), 349–371, 362.

a comprehensively unloving human being, the world would seem empty and absurd. Yet just as a family's dinner table used for daily meals is not merely a piece of wood,[12] likewise the entrance to the home of Gilberte and the Swanns is not exhausted in its meaning by the materials of which it is made. This would suggest that Marcel, in loving, is perhaps *not* out of touch with reality, but better attuned to it in certain respects, by virtue of his infra-red vision.

ii.

When Albertine has just departed from Paris, Marcel finds that his home is haunted by the terrible fact of her absence: the sound of doors being opened, he says, was hurtful "because it was not she that was opening them," and upon returning home he was frequently struck by the lack of Albertine.[13] This void he notes as a tangible feature of the place, as if finding that she was not in the house, or feeling an awareness that she was not in her room (whose door he could not even bear to open), was a genuine discovery. Here we might be reminded of Jean-Paul Sartre's analysis of a situation in which I enter a café to meet my friend Pierre, expecting to find him there, and instead his absence is "a real event concerning this café," whereas the fact that any number of other people I know are not there is *not* phenomenally conspicuous in the same manner.[14] Proust's narrator bears witness to the perceptually experienced content that "Albertine is not present." This is what Scheler would call an "*axiological nuance*" of reality,[15] which gives Marcel reason to be sad—a sadness which itself is based on his love, in the

---

[12] Cf. Martin Heidegger, *Ontology: The Hermeneutics of Facticity*, trans. John van Buren (Bloomington: Indiana University Press, 1999), 69–76.

[13] *The Fugitive*, III: 456–457.

[14] Jean-Paul Sartre, *Being and Nothingness*, trans. Hazel Barnes (New York: Washington Square Press, 1966), 40–42. Cf. Matthew Ratcliffe, *Feelings of Being: Phenomenology, Psychiatry, and the Sense of Reality* (Oxford: Oxford University Press, 2008), 153–154.

[15] Scheler, *Formalism in Ethics and Non-Formal Ethics of Values*, 18.

sense that if not already disposed this way toward her a priori he would not in this manner be pained by her departure. His emotion toward the apartment *sans* Albertine reveals, through his subjectivity, a significant feature of the world.

Although he usually rejects the "material explanation" or the "materialist hypothesis" that life is actually "meaningless" and such an emotion only a distortion or projection,[16] Proust's narrator is also plagued at times by the thought that values may be unreal. This leads him to dismiss his own emotions as merely inner states—the contents "of one's own mind," which are disconnected from the external world.[17] Admittedly, the way in which the apartment and the café contain tables differs from the sense in which Albertine's absence and Pierre's are tangibly *in* those places. The lack of a friend we expected to see is not akin to the volume or mass of a solid object, which any random observer can confirm. It depends more obviously on the structure of our particular subjectivity. Yet the nature of the objective world, insofar as it is knowable by us human beings, arguably cannot be well determined without taking into consideration the contours of the human mind. Proust's narrator sometimes acknowledges that this is the case even for visible objects—for example, when he reflects that:

> the trees, the sun and the sky would not be the same as what we see if they were apprehended by creatures having eyes differently constituted from ours, or else endowed ... with organs other than eyes which would furnish equivalents of trees and sky and sun, though not visual ones.[18]

---

[16] *The Captive*, III: 381–382 and 388. Here, he is discussing Vinteuil's music. On spiritually meaningful versus reductive naturalistic interpretations of music more generally, see also Robert C. Roberts, *Emotions: An Essay in Aid of Moral Psychology* (Cambridge: Cambridge University Press, 2003), 52–54.

[17] *The Fugitive*, III: 568–569. See also III: 656–657, and for analysis see Martha C. Nussbaum, *Love's Knowledge: Essays on Philosophy and Literature* (New York: Oxford University Press, 1990), 271–272.

[18] *The Guermantes Way*, II: 64.

Nevertheless, Marcel is unsure where this Kantian insight leaves us with respect to the world's reality and value, so these issues remain among his constant themes.

iii.

Proust and his narrator seem to hold that we can grasp something *in* the embodied experience of love and suffering, as Marcel learns how much he loves Albertine through the emotional upheavals that he feels after her departure.[19] This knowledge he describes as having just now been brought to him, "hard, glittering, strange, like a crystallized salt, by the abrupt reaction of pain."[20] Earlier in the novel, Marcel likewise finds out what it means that his beloved grandmother is dead, and how much her nonexistence matters to him, precisely by virtue of the overwhelming grief that washes over him all of a sudden when, one year after her death, he reaches down to untie his boots in the same hotel at Balbec where he had previously stayed on a vacation with her. Only in that emotional experience did he learn "that I had lost her forever"; he "clung to this pain, cruel as it was . . . and I longed for the nails that riveted her to my consciousness to be driven yet deeper," for "I knew that if I ever did extract some truth from life, it could only be from such an impression."[21] He knows how terribly sad it is that she will never again

---

[19] On this kind of insight, and its "non-scientific precision," see Nussbaum, *Love's Knowledge*, 255–261. On a variety of truth that is communicated to us "in an impression which is material because it enters us through the senses but yet has a spiritual meaning," see *Time Regained*, III: 912. Regarding the "open wound" of anguish that he begins to feel when he learns that Albertine has gone, a loss of nothing less than his entire life, see *The Fugitive*, III: 425ff. More about this later.

[20] *The Fugitive*, III: 426.

[21] *Cities of the Plain*, II: 785–787 and 790. I discuss this passage in Furtak, *Knowing Emotions*, 69–70 and 181–183. On the way that a feeling of grief can *constitute* a recognition, see also Matthew Ratcliffe, *Real Hallucinations: Psychiatric Illness, Intentionality, and the Interpersonal World* (Cambridge, MA: MIT Press, 2017), 209–217.

return his knocks of greeting on the wall between their rooms. His emotion seems unbearably painful—but "what is painful may nonetheless be true," as Freud points out,[22] and Proust's narrator accepts his grief due to its truthful content.

Needless to say, an episode of grief can last a long time; there is, however, a more basic emotional disposition that must be in place for grief to arise. Here again the notion of the affective a priori is pertinent. We grieve only the loss of those whom we love or care about, and in this sense the most prolonged grief is an emotional response dependent on a more fundamental affective disposition. When a person loves or cares about someone or something, she makes herself vulnerable to being moved by an entire variety of passions[23]—indeed, all that are logically possible. The emotional a priori is implicitly in the background of our encounter with the world, although it is not phenomenally conspicuous at each and every instant. Only as loving or caring beings are we open and receptive to whatever meaning our lives may contain. That is why we could not understand the character of the world without considering the structure of our subjectivity—of our affective capacities especially. It is in this manner that, as Kierkegaard claims, things disclose themselves to the loving subject, and that "to love and to know" are "essentially synonymous."[24] Proust's narrative is evidently concerned with this sort of knowing, even when his narrator is questioning its legitimacy.

---

[22] Sigmund Freud, "On Transience," in *Writings on Art and Literature*, ed. Werner Hamacher and David Wellbery (Stanford, CA: Stanford University Press, 1997), 176–179, 176–177. See also Gilles Deleuze, *Proust and Signs*, trans. Richard Howard (Minneapolis: University of Minnesota Press, 2000), 15–16: "In love . . . it is not pleasure but truth that matters."

[23] See Martha C. Nussbaum, *Upheavals of Thought: The Intelligence of Emotions* (Cambridge: Cambridge University Press, 2001), 71 and 87. See also Harry G. Frankfurt, *The Importance of What We Care About: Philosophical Essays* (Cambridge: Cambridge University Press, 1988), 83. Cf. Scheler, "Ordo Amoris," 101, on how love and interest expose us to being affected.

[24] Søren Kierkegaard, *Papers and Journals: A Selection*, trans. Alastair Hannay (London: Penguin Books, 1996), 343 (*Papirer* IX A 438; *KJN* NB8: 63).

Along these lines, Marcel's pronouncements of indifference, for instance in relation to the departed and then deceased Albertine—"I no longer loved Albertine.... I was suffering from a love that no longer existed"—are proven to be false by the fact that he admits in the same breath that he "felt painfully sad in thinking of her."[25] His sadness demonstrates his underlying love, for we do not feel sadness at having lost someone whom we do not love or care about.[26] Nor do we wish they could still be with us, or compare our aching memory of them to that of an amputee who feels tormented by a phantom limb.[27] It is clear that Marcel is in denial; he is lying to himself (and this is hardly the only time when he will do so). Yet, despite his protests to the contrary, he is well acquainted with the Spinozistic "tendency of everything that exists to prolong its own existence,"[28] and he knows that his well-being has been badly impacted by her loss. Albertine's disappearance, we might say, has moved Proust's narrator from a state of greater to one of lesser perfection.

---

[25] *The Fugitive*, III: 606. Cf. Jennifer Rushworth, *Discourses of Mourning in Dante, Petrarch, and Proust* (Oxford: Oxford University Press, 2016), 94–95.

[26] On how love and care are "never distinguishable" except perhaps by degrees, see Martin Heidegger, *Zollikon Seminars*, trans. Franz Mayr and Richard Askay (Evanston, IL: Northwestern University Press, 2001), 190. Caring is a fundamental mode of being for us, as he notes in numerous places. See, e.g., *Being and Time*, trans. Joan Stambaugh (Albany, NY: SUNY Press, 1996), §§ 41, 43(c), and 69(a). Cf. Giovanna Colombetti, *The Feeling Body: Affective Science Meets the Enactive Mind* (Cambridge, MA: MIT Press, 2014), 18–20. Finally, see Harry G. Frankfurt, *Necessity, Volition, and Love* (Cambridge: Cambridge University Press, 1998), 165: "Loving is a mode of caring," and "among the things that we cannot help caring about are those that we love."

[27] See Merleau-Ponty, *Phenomenology of Perception*, 88–99. Cf. Proust, *The Captive*, III: 334: "I had that vague impression of her that we have of our own limbs"; *The Fugitive*, III: 606: "Thus does an amputee, in certain kinds of weather, feel pain in the limb that he has lost"; *Time Regained*, III: 716.

[28] *Within a Budding Grove*, I: 669. Cf. Baruch Spinoza, *Ethics*, trans. Samuel Shirley (Indianapolis: Hackett Publishing Company, 1992), 108 (Part III, Proposition 6). See also Colombetti, *The Feeling Body*, 6: "The striving being is not indifferent toward its own existence"—it is "interested and concerned." It thus "needs to be open and sensitive to what is conducive to its continuation and what is not." She is explicitly appropriating Spinoza in developing a phenomenology of feeling.

iv.

It may be that we are most accurately aware of anyone or anything when we view him, her, them, or it with an unselfish love that simply wants the beloved to be. This is often described as loving someone as an end rather than a means, or for their own sake.[29] What does Marcel's infra-red vision make him uniquely able to perceive, then? In a word, *possibilities*.[30] The next chapter will be devoted to this topic, yet for now let us observe that the promise of befriending Gilberte Swann initially fills Marcel with longing *because* he learns that she visits cathedrals and castles with her family friend Bergotte, whose writings Proust's narrator has just begun to admire. How sophisticated and intelligent she must be, he thinks, "living in such rare and fortunate circumstances," and what an "unknown life" she must embody for Marcel to know one day.[31] Even her surname starts to seem enchanting to him, just as he will become bedazzled by the entrance of her house. Aware that there is a "believing inherent in perceiving," and that we view someone in light of our notions about him or her,[32] Marcel allows these ideas about Gilberte, all the possibilities she harbors, to influence his conception of her as a potential friend.

Marcel may rejoice in Gilberte's existence, and appreciate her good qualities—of being well-educated, for example, and able to tell him about all the statues in a beautiful town cathedral—in the

---

[29] See, e.g., Max Scheler, *On Feeling, Knowing, and Valuing*, ed. Harold J. Bershady (Chicago: University of Chicago Press, 1992), 153. Cf. Frankfurt, *Necessity, Volition, and Love*, 135.

[30] See Matthew Ratcliffe, *Experiences of Depression: A Study in Phenomenology* (Oxford: Oxford University Press, 2015), 41–79. On how "the possible" is a feature of the world, see Sartre, *Being and Nothingness*, 66–85 and 147–152.

[31] *Swann's Way*, I: 107–108.

[32] I cite Edmund Husserl, *Analyses Concerning Passive and Active Synthesis: Lectures on Transcendental Logic*, trans. Anthony J. Steinbock (Dordrecht: Kluwer Academic Publishers, 2001), 66. Marcel articulates his thesis as follows: "Even the simple act which we describe as 'seeing someone we know' is to some extent an intellectual process," because "we pack the physical outline of the person we see with all the notions we have already formed about him." *Swann's Way*, I: 20.

same manner that a loving and attentive mother could recognize a scarcely discernible aptitude in her child. Yet even if his mode of vision contains the wish that Gilberte be flourishing in her own being, as she is and as she might become, it is *also* colored by his sense that Gilberte could mean something to *him*, could become important in *his* life. In the same way, his grandmother Bathilde is for him a subject in her own right, a kindhearted person who loves being out in the garden even in the rain, and who at Balbec can gaze enraptured at the sea for hours. At the same time, she is, as Marcel knows well, someone whose love for *him* is unbounded. So, his love for Gilberte or for his grandmother is, on the one hand, a mode of awareness that unselfishly celebrates the distinctive being of a person;[33] on the other hand, a way of viewing someone who offers some agreeable possibilities to him in particular. The first is oriented toward what a person *is*, the latter toward what she is or may be *to me*.[34] These ways of seeing sometimes diverge, and nothing troubles Marcel more than this divergence as he asks himself endlessly whether or not he can trust his infra-red vision.

Part of what it means to love or care about anything is that it seems to be worthy of one's attention;[35] and, as José Ortega y Gasset has pointed out, another attribute of loving someone or something is "recognizing and confirming at every moment that they

---

[33] On how love can apprehend less transparently evident good qualities of a person, see John Armstrong, *Conditions of Love: The Philosophy of Intimacy* (New York: W. W. Norton & Company, 2003), 94 and 116–117. Cf. Troy Jollimore, "Love: The Vision View," in *Love, Reason, and Morality*, ed. Esther Engels Kroeker and Katrien Schaubroek (London: Routledge, 2017), 1–19. Regarding love's capacity to "make visible" what is loved, see Jean-Luc Marion, *The Erotic Phenomenon*, trans. Stephen Lewis (Chicago: University of Chicago Press, 2007), 87–88.

[34] Regarding the "unconditional and infinite" love of Marcel's grandmother for him specifically, see Miguel de Beistegui, *Proust as Philosopher: The Art of Metaphor* (London: Routledge, 2012), 62–63. See also Patricia Locke, "Intermittences: Merleau-Ponty and Proust on Time and Grief," in *Chrono-topologies: Hybrid Spatialities and Multiple Temporalities*, ed. Leslie Kavanaugh (Amsterdam: Rodopi, 2010), 147–158, 150.

[35] See, e.g., Bennett Helm, "Love, Identification, and the Emotions," *American Philosophical Quarterly* 46 (2009): 39–59.

are worthy of existence."[36] This appreciative and affirmative love is a disposition that enables us to regard someone in the best light. However, our affective outlook is seldom exclusively charitable and other-oriented. We need not be perniciously self-centered to respond to a loved one in such a way as to be conscious not only of what she or he is, but also of what she or he is to us.

Consider the interest that we might take in a wild bird that we routinely see outside our window.[37] In being concerned for it, we may develop a care for *its* life, and want the creature to be doing well for its own sake. The bird is not linked with any other purposes or hopes of ours, and in this sense our care is admirably unselfish. Yet the image does not adequately capture how we are related to those who hold a special place in our lives. We would be rightly dismayed if these loved ones were to disappear from sight: and we take ourselves to be well within our rights in forming definite expectations of them. Perhaps there is a happy medium somewhere on the spectrum from overly indifferent to overly demanding; at any rate, it is not exemplified by Proust's narrator, who tends toward the latter extreme. He is similar to any other jealously possessive lover, only to a pronounced degree: he confesses to having "an anxious need to be tyrannical" in "matters of love,"[38] and illustrates it continually. His excessive attention to possibilities that only serve his own purposes limits his vision, like that of a man out walking who can only see a park bench as a seat *for himself*, and an approaching person as a rival who might take it.

---

[36] José Ortega y Gasset, *On Love: Aspects of a Single Theme*, trans. Tony Talbot (New York: Meridian Books, 1957), 17.

[37] The inspiration for this touching image of non-possessive love comes from Edward F. Mooney's *Knights of Faith and Resignation* (Albany, NY: SUNY Press, 1991), 53ff. Yet I agree with Sharon Krishek that the image does not fully do justice to how we regard a beloved other. See her *Kierkegaard on Faith and Love* (Cambridge: Cambridge University Press, 2009), 83–85.

[38] This definition of jealousy is from *The Captive*, III: 86. In connection with it, I allude to a classic example from Sartre's *Being and Nothingness*, 341–343. See also Peter Goldie, *The Emotions: A Philosophical Exploration* (Oxford: Oxford University Press, 2000), 232–240.

Furthermore, from early on in the novel Marcel shows the concern that a love, such as Swann's for Odette or his own for Gilberte, may "not correspond to anything outside itself, verifiable by others," our need "to find reasons for [our] passion" leading us to identify after the fact qualities that are "worthy of love," when we do not initially *begin* to love the person for these reasons.[39] This provides Proust's truth-obsessed narrator with yet another reason to doubt his infra-red vision. If the novel as a whole contains "a philosophy of emotions," as has been argued, or even (more ambitiously) "a general theory about minds and their relations with the world,"[40] then it must attempt to answer the question of how the heartfelt affective impressions of a loving subject can perhaps be truth-revealing.

Scheler writes of someone who loved another person "so much that he could not 'observe' her," and Marcel diagnoses himself as suffering from this fault—especially in relation to Albertine.[41] "Love," he seems to lament, is always "partial," and when he attempts to factor out of account his emotional orientation to Albertine he finds that he cannot perceive *anything* about her *due* to his neutrality.[42] In his opinion, he is condemned to being either biased in ways that threaten to distort his vision or else indifferent and hence unaware. Yet we should not too hastily agree with Marcel's judgment: his skepticism, or pessimism, may not be the final word on

---

[39] *Swann's Way*, I: 258 and 444. Cf. Harry G. Frankfurt, *The Reasons of Love* (Princeton, NJ: Princeton University Press, 2004), 38. He writes that, even if "the beloved invariably is ... valuable to the lover," perceiving this value is however not "an indispensable *formative* or *grounding* condition."

[40] The first claim is made by Inge Crosman Wimmers in *Proust and Emotion* (Toronto: University of Toronto Press, 2003), 5; the latter is from Landy's *Philosophy as Fiction*, 9. Italics removed.

[41] Max Scheler, *The Human Place in the Cosmos*, trans. Manfred S. Frings (Evanston, IL: Northwestern University Press, 2009), 34. Cf. Landy, *Philosophy as Fiction*, 89: "As long as he is attached to Albertine, he is too close to see her clearly; once his jealousy has abated, he no longer cares enough to try."

[42] *The Captive*, III: 127. See also *The Captive*, III: 58 and 88. "I should have to cease to love you in order to fix your image," Marcel speculates at one point, yet when "dissociated ... from our emotion whatever it may be, they [beloved women] are only themselves, that is to say next to nothing."

the matter. Before delving further into the Proustian universe, we ought to look further at some reasons for thinking that the affective a priori, constituted by our loves, cares, and concerns, could provide a solid foundation for the apprehension of reality and value. These would afford us grounds for withholding comprehensive skepticism about whether our emotions might be reliable sources of insight—and they would therefore provide a background against which to appraise Marcel's worries about how one's personal affective outlook could be revelatory of the truth, which he remains preoccupied with trying to find. This will accordingly be the task of the following sections.

v.

When we love a concrete individual—a human being, a tradition or a political cause, an intellectual or artistic pursuit, a pet, or anything else that is susceptible of being loved—then we view it as having distinct and inherent worth.[43] We appreciate its qualities, just as Charles Swann is fond of the "purely musical" properties of the sonata phrase with which he falls in love,[44] as it expands his sense of beauty and evokes in him a feeling for "invisible realities in which he had ceased to believe." His response to the little phrase reveals something about Swann's subjectivity, as he is not just a transparent window opening onto the world but a person with a specific aesthetic sensibility. In a way, then, his love for this music shows us something about Swann himself. When the passage from Vinteuil's sonata becomes associated with Swann's romance with Odette, however, he begins to deplore the fact "that it had a meaning of its own, an intrinsic and unalterable beauty," that was extraneous to

---

[43] Cf. Frankfurt, *The Reasons of Love*, 55.
[44] Proust, *Swann's Way*, I: 227–231. On *learning* to love, "not only in music," but also in other cases, see Friedrich Nietzsche, *The Gay Science*, trans. Josefine Nauckhoff (Cambridge: Cambridge University Press, 2001), § 334.

himself and her.[45] It is as if, at this point, Swann wants the musical phrase to have *only* private significance, no longer gesturing toward ideals in which he had almost ceased to believe, but only calling to mind Odette—as we might enjoy remembering a song not for its own sake but only because we happened to hear it while feeling happy on vacation.

Scheler would agree that, in the experience of love, "'higher' values" are "discovered and disclosed" to us.[46] Yet he would add that the truth about the world "is, in a certain sense, a 'personal' truth" due not "to any supposed 'relativity' . . . of the idea of truth," but "to the essential interconnection between person and world."[47] In like manner, Kierkegaard speaks of "an objectivity which takes shape in a corresponding subjectivity,"[48] thus raising the question of how we can understand something as having an existence both *in its own right* and *for us* at the same time. We find Marcel, later in the narrative, wondering what Albertine might be "in herself."[49] With Swann, the type of doubt which tends to arise is uncertainty about whether Odette is worthy of being loved in the way he loves her. While he worries that his love may not quite correspond to "anything outside itself" which is "verifiable by others besides him," he also finds Odette's beauty enhanced by her resemblance to a figure in a favorite painting—and this gives him some reassurance that he is not being duped.[50]

Swann often displays a generous and charitable manner of loving. He grows fond not only of Odette's personal traits, her friends, her opinions, her tastes, indeed "everything that came from her," but he even wishes to *share* these insofar as he can—this is

---

[45] *Swann's Way*, I: 238–239.
[46] Max Scheler, *Formalism in Ethics and Non-Formal Ethics of Values*, 305.
[47] *Formalism in Ethics and Non-Formal Ethics of Values*, 395.
[48] Kierkegaard, *Papers and Journals*, 373 (*Papirer* X 1 A 146; *KJN* NB10: 68). The concept of an "in-itself-for-us" is introduced by Merleau-Ponty in *Phenomenology of Perception*, 375. Italics removed.
[49] *The Captive*, III: 88. See also III: 58, where he asks the same question about Albertine and Andrée both at once.
[50] *Swann's Way*, I: 258 and I: 244–245.

"a task so attractive that he tried to find enjoyment in the things she liked," locating in them a "charm" that seems "mysterious," yet enchanting.[51] He wants to apprehend the beauty of whatever has a place in her world. One might suppose that he views even her chronic fault-finding in an appreciative and forgiving light.[52] He wishes her to be nothing other than what she is. Aside from the question of how consistently Swann succeeds at maintaining this kind of other-centered loving attention, it deserves to be investigated more closely.

vi.

In portraying love as a certain way of seeing, Iris Murdoch has advocated a "just and loving gaze directed upon an individual reality" as the best way of viewing a person as he or she is *and* in the most favorable light available:[53] love is therefore a way of being attentive to someone or something, perceiving what uniquely defines the beloved. Swann cares about Odette's life and well-being, regarding her not as an instantiation of a universal category or as a "thoroughfare for an impersonal rational activity,"[54] but as a distinctive and irreplaceable being. When it takes this form, love is *not* a desire to project "non-existent perfections" onto another, substituting our own fantasies for her concrete actuality:[55] that

---

[51] *Swann's Way*, I: 268–270.

[52] For a brief account of how Odette finds fault with everything from Swann's neighborhood to his upholstery, see *Swann's Way*, I: 266–267. She exemplifies precisely the contrary—uncharitable, i.e., unloving—mode of vision. On the difference between "become what thou art" and "thou shouldst be thus and thus," see Max Scheler, *The Nature of Sympathy*, trans. Peter Heath (New Haven, CT: Yale University Press, 1954), 159–161.

[53] See, e.g., Murdoch, *Existentialists and Mystics: Writings on Philosophy and Literature*, ed. Peter Conradi (London: Penguin Books, 1999), 327; see also pages 215–216, where she claims that love is "the discovery of reality," the "apprehension of something else, something particular, as existing outside us."

[54] Scheler, *Formalism in Ethics and Non-Formal Ethics of Values*, 372–373; see also Frankfurt, *The Reasons of Love*, 79–80.

[55] Ortega y Gasset, *On Love*, 21–22. Kierkegaard also defends the notion that genuine love is "an honest . . . vision of concrete individuals, focusing on them 'as they

would have the effect of keeping us out of touch with the world. And we do tend to be dismayed when someone who *would* love us has a radically inaccurate conception of who we are, failing to recognize what distinguishes us in our particularity—an unmistakable sign that we ordinarily differentiate between how one is viewed by some other subject and how one *is*, full stop.

Insofar as Swann *does* love Odette as she is, rather than as he wants or imagines her to be, he allows her to become a real, valuable being in his awareness. Her existence matters to him as a feature of *his* realm of concern, and in loving her he affirms the meaning of *her* life, which is independent of his. To love is thus "to will to exist" for "each one individually," as Kierkegaard claims.[56] By doing so we extend our affective range of contact with the world, as its aspects impinge upon our hearts. Our emotional vantage point is enhanced *and* made more complicated by these loves, because we are susceptible to being upset for better or worse by contingencies that relate to what we love and care about. That is why a beloved person has "the power to cause us so much suffering or happiness,"[57] as Odette does to Swann.

The well-attuned lover is therefore oriented toward the beloved, a non-fabricated being, in such a way that his picture of her (or hers of him) is not falsified by distortions or fantastic impositions. He envisions her as what she is, a person for whom a world exists,[58]

---

are' rather than trimmed to our measure." M. Jamie Ferreira, *Love's Grateful Striving* (New York: Oxford University Press, 2001), 116; see also Krishek, *Kierkegaard on Faith and Love*, 156.

[56] Søren Kierkegaard, *Works of Love*, trans. Howard V. Hong and Edna H. Hong (Princeton, NJ: Princeton University Press, 1995), 83–84. See also page 67, on "loving each one individually" with an other-focused outlook that "is not proudly independent of its object." On how a person's loves and cares define his or her "range of contact with the universe," see Scheler, "Ordo Amoris," 111. Italics removed.

[57] Proust, *Swann's Way*, I: 257. A pessimist would count this as one of many threads that keep us bound to the world, tugging on us with painful emotions of every variety, and the pessimist would not be wrong.

[58] Cf. Troy Jollimore, *Love's Vision* (Princeton, NJ: Princeton University Press, 2001), 25–26 and 123–125.

owner of an utterly singular perspective through which a unique truth can be disclosed. His love for her enables him to glimpse even possibilities that have yet to manifest themselves, as far as anyone else can judge. Moreover, this love is not to be mistaken for a purely inner sensation associated with the idea of an external cause:[59] we can improve on the philosophical premises that would lead us to accept that impoverished notion of love's intentionality.

Or can we? Widespread, although nihilistic, habits of thought can influence us to question at times—in certain moods, let us say—whether the apparent beauty and significance of what we love is merely illusory. We know very well that we do not experience ourselves as actively bequeathing onto beloved objects those same qualities we love *in* them. When Marcel witnesses and is astounded by the extraordinary green color of Andrée's eyes,[60] that color is in *her* eyes, not his. He is relying on ordinary, not infra-red, vision. On the other hand, as he becomes increasingly drawn to the soul that peers out at him from Albertine's laughing, sparkling, bright, brilliant, smiling eyes, her mysterious appeal is something "more" that goes beyond her visible eye color.[61] "From the depths of what universe did she discern me?"[62] he wonders, conceding that her subjective vantage point was the center of a world other than his own. To be truly skeptical about Albertine's existence as another minded being akin to himself would be to negate the reality and value of human experience and to accept a meaningless view of

---

[59] "Is what or who[m] we love merely the cause arising somewhere of a state arising in us, a state we transfer onto what we call our beloved?" Martin Heidegger asks this question in *The Fundamental Concepts of Metaphysics: World, Finitude, Solitude*, trans. William McNeill and Nicholas Walker (Bloomington: Indiana University Press, 1995), 89–90. Cf. Spinoza, *Ethics*, 112 (Part III, "Scholium" to Proposition 14).

[60] *Within a Budding Grove*, I: 943. Seeing her eye color is depicted as like seeing "a glimpse, through an open door in a dark house, of a room into which the sun is shining with a greenish reflection from the glittering sea."

[61] *Within a Budding Grove*, I: 850, I: 852, I: 974, and I: 981. Jean-Luc Marion remarks on how "the gaze of the other . . . remains invisible," at the heart of "the blackness and the emptiness of the pupil." See "What Love Knows," in *Prolegomena to Charity*, trans. Stephen Lewis (New York: Fordham University Press, 2002), 153–169, 167.

[62] *Within a Budding Grove*, I: 851.

things: one to which Marcel is sometimes drawn, although there is also evidence that he knows better. "Loving helps us to discern, to discriminate," he says when observing how he is able to distinguish Albertine's voice from those of the other young women.[63] Love can in this way make a person not blind, but perceptive—even perspicuous.

At least, it *can*. Admittedly, Marcel never ceases to entertain the hypothesis that, because "the truth is so variable for each of us" as subjects, and the objects of our love not only "change in relation to ourselves" but "change also in themselves," the beloved other might *in herself* be not so very meaningful as she appears to us.[64] When he has adopted this theoretical stance, he is in agreement with the view of William James that "the passion of love" illustrates how what we see as meaningful only seems this way due to "pure gifts" bestowed by our minds onto "our respective worlds."[65] Yet if another person's soul were nothing but our own invention, then she or he could not conceal anything from us, and we could not run up as Marcel does against "that unknowable thing" that "another person's life invariably is to us."[66] If we grant that the beloved is *not* our invention or projection, and that people can indeed be bound together in a relationship—not only *with ropes*—then it follows by entailment that there can be such a thing as threats to a relationship, and hence grounds for jealousy.[67] And we are unlikely to apprehend such a threat unless we occupy the emotionally engaged standpoint of a loving person.

---

[63] *Within a Budding Grove*, I: 969.

[64] Proust, *The Captive*, III: 12 and III: 63. On the beloved "in herself" see, e.g., *The Captive*, III: 88. Regarding the continual change in observer as well as what is observed, see Peter Jones, *Philosophy and the Novel* (Oxford: Oxford University Press, 1975), 175.

[65] William James, *The Varieties of Religious Experience* (New York: Vintage Books, 1990), 141.

[66] *The Captive*, III: 56.

[67] On jealousy, see Cheshire Calhoun, "Subjectivity and Emotion," in *Thinking about Feeling*, ed. Solomon, 107–121, 109. As for how people can be bound not only by material bonds see Paul Grice, *The Conception of Value* (New York: Oxford University Press, 2001), 44–45.

Although what we see depends in part on our way of seeing, an insight that will be explored in greater depth as we move forward, our position is not that of almighty world-makers superimposing value onto a blank screen. It is because he tries to account for both sides of this story that Proust's narrator undergoes some vacillation from one philosophical extreme to the other. When emphasizing the objectivity of love, he recognizes the kind of affective knowledge we gain when we become acquainted with another person, in their actual existence and as they might possibly become. What we thereby love and know is the specific particularity of the beloved. As Scheler claims, "the act of loving" discloses an "individual personality," which is what is known by the one who loves.[68] Nor is it lamentable that as finite beings we are inevitably *partial* with respect to what we love. In some moods, however, Marcel continues to be troubled by the fact that affective perception is shaped by one's idiosyncratic perspective, and therefore contestable. This is evinced by statements such as that "love places in a person who is loved what exists only in the person who loves,"[69] a reflection on his own experience that prompts Marcel to mention Robert de Saint-Loup's love for Rachel.

Things appear different to differently oriented observers, and this has been cited since classical times as a reason for suspending judgment as to what is the case, or concluding that knowledge is not attainable. A host of other characters, including Marcel, believe that Saint-Loup is suffering from an illusion simply due to his view of Rachel as she appears through loving eyes: to him, she seems to be a glamorous actress, a fascinating woman to whom he is irresistibly drawn. Rachel, for him, is someone "whose personality ... occupied incessantly his toiling imagination," an intriguingly mysterious woman whom "he felt that he would never really know."[70] How,

---

[68] Max Scheler, *The Nature of Sympathy*, 166–167. See also Jean-Luc Marion, *The Erotic Phenomenon*, 79.
[69] *Time Regained*, III: 950–951.
[70] *The Guermantes Way*, II: 160–162. See also, e.g., *The Guermantes Way*, II: 233–234.

the others ask, could he have fallen in love with her? For those who do not love her regard Rachel as merely a cheap prostitute, devoid of inherent worth. And it is true that at one time she worked in a brothel. Yet are we therefore justified in concluding that "Rachel the tart was more real than the other," and that Saint-Loup was making a perceptual error?[71] What we are faced with here is not necessarily a contrast between the one accurate view of Rachel, as seen by an unloving onlooker, and an alternative vantage point which is deluded. If we take seriously the idea that the lover might *not* be just getting a worse view of the same thing which the cold eye of reason "would discern more clearly," as Scheler encourages us to do,[72] then we must find it cynical to presume that a woman is most adequately apprehended by someone who regards her as nothing but a prostitute.

vii.

The specificity of love's focus means that there is no equivalent and can be no substitute for the beloved. Their "sheer particularity" is what we love,[73] which is why they are irreplaceable—as opposed to just instantiating a general type. It is not as *a* woman that Rachel is loved by Saint-Loup, but emphatically as *this* woman. By virtue of

---

[71] *The Guermantes Way*, II: 164; Marcel wonders whether *or not* this perspective on Rachel reveals who she truly is. According to Vincent Descombes, Robert is simply mistaken, whereas Marcel "knows better." *Proust: Philosophy of the Novel*, trans. Catherine Macksey (Stanford, CA: Stanford University Press, 1992), 267–269. Landy suggests, more plausibly, that *both* impressions of Rachel probably capture "facets or potentialities of her complex being." *Philosophy as Fiction*, 61–63. Cf. İngrid Vendrell Ferran, *Die Vielfalt der Erkenntnis: Eine Analyse des Kognitiven Werts der Literatur* (Paderborn: mentis, 2018), 191.

[72] Scheler, *The Nature of Sympathy*, 150. Cf. Jollimore, *Love's Vision*, 53: love affords "a way of seeing the world that makes possible insights and understandings that cannot be achieved through . . . more dispassionate modes of engagement." Later, the roles will be reversed, when it is Saint-Loup who cannot grasp what Marcel sees in Albertine. *The Fugitive*, III: 445ff.

[73] Harry Frankfurt, *Taking Ourselves Seriously and Getting It Right*, ed. Debra Satz (Stanford, CA: Stanford University Press, 2006), 40.

loving in this manner, we form a definite sense of what interests us, what matters in our world, out of the much vaster realm of all that a person might love. Hence the affirmation of a loved one's existence, the wish for his or her well-being, can be described as simultaneously an acknowledgment of another *and* a revealing expression of one's own affective standpoint. Our loves define who we are. When we "directly experience the positive value of a being other than ourselves," and thereby gain an "appreciation for the uniqueness and irreplaceability of that being,"[74] his or her intrinsic significance becomes a site of terminal value for us. In this manner, love brings us into touch with elements of the world, enabling us to discover and feel convinced of the reality and meaning of what is not oneself. Saint-Loup by loving Rachel, Swann by loving Odette, and Marcel by loving first Gilberte and then Albertine, find that life has become significantly clarified but also made more potentially upsetting due to their loves. It is no wonder if they sometimes exhibit ambivalence about these attachments. A loving subject's fortune is inherently unstable.

When we succeed at loving in such a way as to find joy in another person's distinct existence—his or her way of seeing and feeling, of acting and responding, of having a history and imagination as well as a perspective on the world, none of which are identical to our own—we embrace and affirm a radical otherness, comprising differences that transcend our understanding. The vulnerability and risk involved in doing so expose us to precarious insecurity: a finite, separate person is uncontrolled by us, and our love for them extends the realm of what matters to us and is liable to lead to emotional upheaval. For Swann, at one stage, the domain of what is *not* indifferent to him coincides exactly

---

[74] Ralph Ellis, *Love and the Abyss: An Essay on Finitude and Value* (Chicago: Open Court Publishing, 2004), 22. As for why the other person's "*truth*" is established through a history of striving and struggle, see Peter J. Hadreas, *A Phenomenology of Love and Hate* (Burlington, VT: Ashgate, 2007), 28.

with what pertains to Odette,[75] and Marcel through his love for Albertine takes an interest in "all the points in space and time that [she] has occupied and will occupy," everything that is connected with her life.[76] In each case, so much of the man's own well-being depends on the beloved woman. To love another finite human being, as he or she changes over time, is to be in an uncertain predicament: what he or she does, what he or she *is*, affects us. So, too, does anything that impacts him or her, insofar as we suffer through his or her sufferings as well. In both ways, love leads to painful emotions.

Yet if love has a logic of its own, then the very exclusiveness of its vision may provide us with access to a kind of truth which it alone can reveal. Failures to apprehend someone whom we love, such as when she is seen through the lens of whatever we *want* from her, would then need to be classified as contingent and evitable failings of an affective capacity that *aims* at disclosing the person as she is. And Marcel would be correct in claiming that love "helps us to discern" in anyone "the unique portrait of her individuality."[77] Love could then be truthful if it is attentive to the distinctiveness of the beloved, opening our eyes to his or her particularity—that of a unique, never identically duplicated, vantage point and way of being.[78] Embodied in each case is a subject of experience who loves and cares as no other person does. The love of human beings must necessarily be incomplete, due to the unfinished nature of every beloved. Yet even if we never quite grasp the *Ding an sich* of another's

---

[75] See, e.g., *Swann's Way*, I: 351. He finds himself "in a state of melancholy indifference to everything that did not concern Odette."

[76] *The Captive*, III: 95. For Marcel, the wish to know and the wish to own are invariably linked, even if his desire to *understand* the beloved is genuine in its own right.

[77] Again, see *Within a Budding Grove*, I: 969. See also *The Captive*, III: 258, on "the irreducibly individual existence of the soul."

[78] See Kierkegaard, *Works of Love*, 270–272. As Clément Rosset adds in *Joyful Cruelty*, trans. David F. Bell (Oxford: Oxford University Press, 1993), 87–94, existential truth is by its very nature subject to doubt: "If uncertainty is cruel, it is because the need for certainty is urgent," such that within each passionate believer "is a skeptic who is unhappy and ashamed to be one."

subjectivity, it is solely through love that we are introduced, partially, to the unique meaning of a person's life. In his quest for truth, Marcel must rely upon an epistemic standpoint that is fallible, but not blind. His reasons for questioning the way things appear through his infra-red vision do not offer Proust's ultimate conclusion on the topic.

2
On Possibility and Significance

i.

Alluding to Stendhal, Proust's narrator suggests that beauty is appealing because it affords us "a promise of happiness,"[1] hinting at something valuable that remains to be unveiled. And one of Marcel's characteristic attunements is toward what might be called *possibilities for romantic encounter*. Even when these are directed toward a promise of mere superficial gratification, as he imagines himself pursuing with the chambermaid of Madame Putbus, his attentive regard for her includes some speculation about the "unknown quantity" that her mind represents to him.[2] When his gaze is inclined toward Mademoiselle de Stermaria, the mysteries of her subjectivity evoke a more complex poetic account:

> From a certain look which flooded for a moment the wells—instantly dry again—of her eyes, a look in which one sensed that almost humble docility which the predominance of a taste for sensual pleasures gives to the proudest of women, who will soon come to recognize but one form of personal magic, that which any man will enjoy in her eyes who can make her feel those pleasures, an actor or a mountebank for whom, perhaps, she will one day leave her husband, and from a certain pink tinge, warm and sensual, which flushed her pallid cheeks, like the color

---

[1] *The Captive*, III: 136.
[2] See *Cities of the Plain*, II: 779–781.

that stained the hearts of the white water-lilies in the Vivonne, I thought I could discern that she might readily have consented to my coming to seek in her the savor of that life of poetry and romance which she led in Brittany, a life [that] she held enclosed in her body.[3]

Here, we see that the sedimented history this woman embodies also gestures ahead, in the manner of an overture to possibilities not yet disclosed. Likewise with the girl he glimpses on the old bridge in Carqueville, who has "a more serious and a more self-willed air" than other young women in the village and has evidently been spending the day fishing:

She had a tanned complexion, soft eyes but with a look of contempt for her surroundings, and a small nose, delicately and attractively modeled. My eyes alighted upon her skin; and my lips, at a pinch, might have believed that they had followed my eyes. But it was not only to her body that I should have liked to attain; it was also the person that lived inside it, and with which there is but one form of contact, namely to attract its attention, but one sort of penetration, to awaken an idea in it.

And this inner being of the handsome fisher-girl seemed to be still closed to me. . . . I could have wished that the idea of me which entered this being and took hold in it should bring me not merely her attention but her admiration . . . and should compel her to keep me in her memory until the day when I should be able to meet her again.[4]

---

[3] *Within a Budding Grove*, I: 740–741.
[4] *Within a Budding Grove*, I: 769–770. On "experiencing the possible," see Ratcliffe, *Feelings of Being*, 121–130 and *Real Hallucinations*, 123–124. See also Husserl, *Analyses Concerning Passive and Active Synthesis*, 91, regarding the "horizon" of possibilities, and "alternative possibilities," which in an important sense "are there" in the experienced world.

Again, the perception of another person can be charged with a sense of a potential for romance, her skin as *perhaps to be kissed by me*, and in each case the exotic (and hence intriguing) depths that she harbors of consciousness and personality, which I might explore—along with the capacity for scorn or admiration of me. In this manner, one's affective comportment toward the world is an attunement, an emotional orientation, toward the possibilities that it holds. The author of Kierkegaard's pseudonymous "Seducer's Diary" would concur: "How boldly and saucily she looks around the world," he observes of a lovely young girl who appears "more tempting, more seductive" when the "puffing of the wind" reveals "the beauty of her form"; it has the ability to blow her hat off into his hands, making him into the "lucky fellow" who is obliged to return it to her.[5] "Good days are coming now," he predicts, noting the element of chance in his favorable fortune, and (concerning the girl) thinking of "her hope, her future."

As J. Hillis Miller points out, a "recurrent motif" in Proust's novel is that, in our actual lives no less than in literary works of art, we are given a "hint that there must be an immense proliferation of possible worlds."[6] This includes the many universes to which human eyes open from their various perspectives, on which Marcel repeatedly comments and about which much more remains to be said, but also events that *might have been*, such as having met Albertine earlier than he in fact did. In retrospect, declining an invitation to join his father at a dinner party where he knew Albertine (of whom he had heard) would be present takes on a significance unknown to Marcel at the time. As he reflects:

> So it is that the different periods of our life overlap with one another. We scornfully decline, because of one whom we love and

---

[5] *Either/Or, Volume I*, trans. Howard Hong and Edna Hong (Princeton, NJ: Princeton University Press, 1987), 354–359. This girl looks "so exuberant, so full of longing and anticipation," i.e., as containing her own wealth of possibility.

[6] J. Hillis Miller, *On Literature* (London: Routledge, 2002), 64.

who will some day be of so little account, to see another who is of no account to-day, whom we shall love to-morrow, whom we might perhaps, had we consented to see her now, have loved a little sooner and who would thus have put a term to our present sufferings, bringing others, it is true, in their place.[7]

Sufferings related to Marcel's love (at the time) for Gilberte might have been replaced by a set of sufferings different from what he actually experiences in relation to Albertine after meeting her later. So, his love affair with Albertine might have been another story entirely, one that could possibly have had a less tragic—or at least a differently tragic—end.

ii.

Proust's narrator is by turns fascinated and tormented by the knowledge that his loves were shaped by contingent factors, and that they might have transpired in other ways than they did: "whoever it is who has determined the course of our life has, in so doing, excluded all the lives which we might have led instead."[8] The abiding reality of these alternative worlds renders plausible a rather extravagant ontology:

It is uncontroversially true that things might be otherwise than they are. I believe, and so do you, that things could have been different in countless ways. But what does this mean? Ordinary language permits the paraphrase: there are many ways things could have been besides the way they actually are. On the face of it, this sentence is an existential quantification. It says that there

---

[7] *Within a Budding Grove*, I: 674. See also Landy, *Philosophy as Fiction*, 121: "The nonevent" of Marcel's missing this early opportunity to meet Albertine "has *become* something worth talking about."
[8] *Time Regained*, III: 955.

exist many entities of a certain description, to wit "ways things could have been." ... I therefore believe in the existence of entities that might be called "ways things could have been." I prefer to call them "possible worlds."[9]

However we may conceive of the metaphysical status of possibilities, we must agree that in our existence they have an experiential reality: indeed, without them many of the emotions we routinely feel could not arise. At one point Saint-Loup reminds Marcel of a philosophical book they read together, about "the richness of the world of possibilities compared with the real world."[10] This means that all the alternative ways in which Marcel's relationship with Albertine might have unfolded vastly outnumber the one way it actually does. If he is haunted by a sense of how things might have been otherwise, there will always be an abundant supply of these ghosts to be tormented by.

For the present tense is not only filled to overflowing with the past. It is also "big with the future," as Leibniz attests.[11] What a phenomenologist might designate as a "horizon of possibilities" or "a field of possibilities"[12] is present at each moment in Proust's novel when his narrator first encounters any of the *jeunes filles* that set his imagination whirling. Marcel explains such an encounter in terms of an organic "desire to live which is reborn in us whenever we become conscious anew of beauty," and of all the potential that it seems to

---

[9] David K. Lewis, *Counterfactuals* (Cambridge, MA: Harvard University Press, 1973), 84.

[10] *The Guermantes Way*, II: 115. Robert Gordon classifies an emotion such as hope as an "epistemic" rather than a "factive" emotion, because it is about what *might* be rather than what *is* the case: see *The Structure of Emotions* (Cambridge: Cambridge University Press, 1987), 26–27.

[11] Gottfried Wilhelm Leibniz, *Theodicy*, trans. E. M. Huggard (New Haven, CT: Yale University Press, 1952), 341. This caught Kierkegaard's attention around the time he was writing the first few pages of *Repetition*.

[12] See, e.g., Merleau-Ponty, *Phenomenology of Perception*, 156n and 188. Cf. Edmund Husserl, *Ideas II*, trans. Richard Rojcewicz and André Schuwer (Dordrecht: Kluwer Academic Publishers, 1989), 38–42 and 72.

hold.[13] It is because they are brimming with enticing possibilities that the girls have the power to renew his wish to be alive. Needless to say, the sense of possibility they awaken in him is passionately felt: it has a tangible emotional valence. Just as the enthralling Mademoiselle de Stermaria seems to embody a hidden life of poetry and romance, any new face that captivates Marcel represents a friend who may be made, an unknown subject with her own passions and aspirations and individual outlook on the world, who may be someone with whom to fall in love. The beauty of a person indicates a concealed good to be perhaps discovered; in being moved by that person's beauty, he yearns for more of this good thing in his life.

In one enchanted passage, Proust's narrator bursts out with an enthusiastic apostrophe to *jeunes filles*, in the following words: "O girls, O successive rays in the swirling vortex wherein we throb with emotion on seeing you reappear while barely recognizing you, in the dizzy velocity of light. . . . O drops of gold, always dissimilar and always surpassing our expectation!"[14] Part of what intoxicates Marcel, in this little hymn of praise, is that the young women are (1) each singular and unlike any other, and (2) filled with possibilities that cannot be anticipated in advance of being revealed. On his rides in the countryside with his grandmother and Madame de Villeparisis, he repeatedly catches sight of incarnate possibilities from every social class and of every description, girls about whom he says that, "from the day on which I had first known that their cheeks could be kissed, I had become curious about their souls," and as a result "the universe had appeared to me more interesting."[15] Here, Marcel's orientation to existence is typified above all

---

[13] *Within a Budding Grove*, I: 705. Cf. Alexander Nehamas, *Only a Promise of Happiness* (Princeton, NJ: Princeton University Press, 2007), 129–130: "Even the narrowest judgment of beauty has far-reaching consequences," because "you can't know in advance the sort of person it will make you. . . . To think of beauty as only a promise of happiness is [thus] to be willing to live with ineradicable uncertainty."
[14] *The Captive*, III: 58–59.
[15] *Within a Budding Grove*, I: 764–766.

by an alertness to a certain kind of possibility;[16] his world harbors romantic prospects just as plainly as a thundercloud harbors the likelihood of rain. His condition is one in which, as he says, "we desire, we seek, we see Beauty."[17]

This is how he is disposed or attuned at the instant when he sees for the first time Albertine and her "little band" of friends walking along the esplanade on the Balbec shore. As one critic has observed, literary works of art are especially adept at conveying "atmospheres and moods," which "belong to the substance and reality of the world."[18] No abbreviated account can do justice to the eleven remarkable pages describing the narrator's initial impressions of the little band, and his heightened sense of all the enticing possibilities to be (perhaps) disclosed, yet this excerpt is representative of the whole:

> The girls whom I had noticed, with the control of gesture that comes from the perfect suppleness of one's own body and a sincere contempt for the rest of humanity, were advancing straight ahead, without hesitation or stiffness, performing exactly the movements that they wished to perform, each of their limbs completely independent of the others, the rest of the body preserving that immobility which is so noticeable in good waltzers.... They were known to me only by a pair of hard, obstinate and mocking eyes, for instance, or by cheeks whose pinkness had a coppery tint reminiscent of geraniums; and even these features I had not yet indissolubly attached to any one of these girls rather than another; and when (according to the order in which the group

---

[16] That it takes no more than a momentary glance for his curiosity to awaken, as in the case of the girl who emerges from the train station at a stop on the way to Balbec, shows how glaring this attunement is in Marcel: *Within a Budding Grove*, I: 705–707. On how possibilities exist not as mere thoughts, although not without subjects, see Sartre, *Being and Nothingness*, 150–151.

[17] *Within a Budding Grove*, I: 845.

[18] Hans Ulrich Gumbrecht, *Atmosphere, Mood, Stimmung*, trans. Erik Butler (Stanford, CA: Stanford University Press, 2012), 12 and 20, italics removed.

met the eye, marvelous because the most different aspects were juxtaposed, because all the color scales were combined in it, but confused as a piece of music in which I was unable to isolate and identify at the moment of their passage the successive phrases, no sooner distinguished than forgotten) I saw a pallid oval, black eyes, green eyes, emerge, I did not know if these were the same that had already charmed me a moment ago, [for] I could not relate them to any one girl whom I had set apart from the rest and identified.[19]

Soon he begins to differentiate the members of the group, even though there continues to be "between their independent and separate bodies" an "invisible but harmonious bond, like a single warm shadow, a single atmosphere, making of them a whole as homogeneous in its parts as it was different from the crowd through which their procession gradually wound."[20] Although he compares their beauty to the beauty of flowers, reminding us of the younger Marcel's love for the hawthorn blossoms, what he finds most attractive about the girls is the unknown depths of subjectivity they embody: "if we thought that the eyes of such a girl were merely two glittering sequins of mica, we should not be athirst to know her." However, "we sense that what shines in those reflecting discs is not due solely to their material composition."[21] Rather, it is their ideas and their plans, their desires, sympathies and aversions, as well as the entire sedimented history of places they have been, friends they

---

[19] *Within a Budding Grove*, I: 847. The passage is marked throughout by what one commentator calls "the affect of possibility," namely "amazement." Rok Bencin, "*'Sans Cause'*: Affect and Truth in Marcel Proust," *Filozofski Vestnik* 38, no. 3 (2017): 53–66, 59. It also exemplifies the "insatiable curiosity about the alterity of the other" that distinguishes Proustian desire, as Emmanuel Levinas points out: see *Proper Names*, trans. Michael B. Smith (Stanford, CA: Stanford University Press, 1996), 103.

[20] *Within a Budding Grove*, I: 850–851.

[21] *Within a Budding Grove*, I: 851–852. On Scheler's view of how a beloved's inward being "flashes forth," intimating more than is immediately given, see A. R. Luther, *Persons in Love: A Study of Max Scheler's "Wesen und Formen der Sympathie"* (The Hague: Martinus Nijhoff Publishers, 1972), 112.

have made, and homes to which they will return—all of which he thirsts for, as "a parched land burns" for water, in longing to get to know them.[22] Never before, he claims, did he see "anything so beautiful," replete "with so much that was unknown, so inestimably precious, so apparently inaccessible."[23] Marcel is drawn to them due in part to their undisclosed qualities, which he *almost* glimpses in feeling that each of them is more than is yet shown; the significant fortuity of being located where he was at the moment they walked past is lucky for him, although it offers only a promise of happiness.

"A man sees only what concerns him," Thoreau writes, explaining how perception is shaped by the constitution of the perceiver.[24] And, no doubt, an indifferent observer nearby might fail even to notice the group of young women walking along the esplanade. Marcel's emotional disposition renders him receptive to being impressed by them, allowing him to grasp and appreciate specific features of his world. Later on, he will view the roads in the area as "simply the means of rejoining Albertine," because for him they do have this promise, just as a cube-shaped object holds the possibility of displaying other sides that are currently unseen.[25] In this manner, we see how a response to the world is filtered through the lens of one's subjectivity: deprived of that meaning, those roads would actually *look* different. Remarking on this phenomenon, Scheler notes that as our "attitudes of interest and love" create in us

---

[22] *Within a Budding Grove*, I: 852–853. He finds extremely appealing, and yet unlikely, "the supposition that I might some day be the friend of one or other of these girls, that these eyes, whose incomprehensible gaze struck me from time to time and played unwittingly upon me like an effect of sunlight on a wall, might ever, by some miraculous alchemy, allow the idea of my existence, some affection for my person, to interpenetrate their ineffable particles."

[23] *Within a Budding Grove*, I: 855. Cf. Nicholas Rescher, *Luck* (Pittsburgh: University of Pittsburgh Press, 1995), 64. See also Nehamas, *Only a Promise of Happiness*, 63: we sense beauty in what a person has not yet manifested.

[24] Henry David Thoreau, "Autumnal Tints," in *Collected Essays and Poems*, ed. Elizabeth H. Witherell (New York: Library of America, 2001), 367–395, 394.

[25] *Cities of the Plain*, II: 1044–1045; on the cube, see Merleau-Ponty, *Phenomenology of Perception*, 308. Marcel yearns to know "what was inside Albertine," but realizes that she is inexhaustible: *The Fugitive*, III: 555.

"a readiness for being affected," our felt sense of what is significant is "peculiar to each" of us.[26] When Proust's narrator loses interest in communicating with a person, it is because she no longer seems to contain, "like a nest of boxes, all the possibilities" for encounter,[27] and for becoming an important part of his life, which she once did. What he tends to describe as the death of a self that loved another particular human being could equally well be termed the loss of a world in which this other subject teems with possibilities, in a way that is relevant to him.

iii.

There is a sad kind of self-doubt that troubles Marcel at such moments as when he composes a letter to Gilberte, no longer loved by him, and is astonished that he can now write her name with utter calm, "without emotion, and as though finishing off a boring school essay," when earlier he had passionately written her name all over page after page of his notebooks.[28] Skeptical once more of his infra-red vision, he reflects that perhaps at the time he loved her she had simply been illuminated by a glow that emanated from inside *him*. It is similar to when a person is in a disenchanted mood and, unable to step outside of it, questions how the world had ever seemed to contain anything worth hoping for, pursuing, or even avoiding. Everything now appears weary, stale, flat, and worthless:[29] therefore, one reasons, perhaps the value with which things

---

[26] Scheler, "Ordo Amoris," 101 and 107.
[27] *The Guermantes Way*, II: 378–379. On his loss of interest in Gilberte and, hence, the death of the self that loved her see, e.g., *Cities of the Plain*, II: 739 and *The Captive*, III: 92.
[28] *Cities of the Plain*, II: 765–766.
[29] Echoing Hamlet, Simon Blackburn notes that for those in certain affective states the world at present simply *is* "weary, stale, flat, and unprofitable." See *Ruling Passions* (Oxford: Clarendon Press, 1998), 8–9 and 131. On how one form of skeptical doubt about axiological matters "is the view that there is really nothing worth caring about," see Frankfurt, *The Importance of What We Care About*, 91n. Cf. Ratcliffe, *Experiences of Depression*, 276–280. "Error theory," in this realm, is represented, e.g., by Angela

once seemed to be animated was just an illusion, an "error" as some theorists would say. Proust's narrator never entirely ceases to be tempted by this line of thought, and to wonder if—as a common cliché suggests—one's moods lend a false coloring to what is, in reality, a colorless world, a feeling of value and meaning to a dull heap of insignificant matter.[30]

As relatively trivial a modification of subjectivity as fatigue, dizziness, or nausea can be lived through as a pervasive atmosphere,[31] enhancing the sense that our disposition is highly variable and maybe thus untrustworthy. Marcel notices how much his emotional comportment has altered after drinking himself into a state of general "euphoria" (supposedly for medical reasons) on the train to Balbec:

> When at the first stop I clambered back into our compartment I told my grandmother how pleased I was to be going to Balbec, that I felt that everything would go off splendidly, that... the train was most comfortable, the barman and the attendants so friendly that I should like to make the journey often so as to have the opportunity of seeing them again.[32]

Finding him in this amiable mood, Marcel's grandmother just looks at him with concern and suggests that he try to take a nap. But instead, he soon finds himself staring in awe at the blue window-blind:

Mendelovici in *The Phenomenal Basis of Intentionality* (Oxford: Oxford University Press, 2018).

[30] Apparently endorsing the cliché is Roberts in *Emotions*, 112–115; urging us to question it is Stephen Mulhall, in "Can There Be an Epistemology of Moods?," *Royal Institute of Philosophy Supplement* 41 (1996): 191–210.

[31] Dan Zahavi, *Self-Awareness and Alterity: A Phenomenological Investigation* (Evanston, IL: Northwestern University Press, 1999), 125. See also Heidegger on *soma* and *psyche*: *Zollikon Seminars*, 76–80. Cf. Ratcliffe, *Feelings of Being*, 106–129 and *Experiences of Depression*, 75–91.

[32] *Within a Budding Grove*, I: 700–701.

The contemplation of this blind appeared to me an admirable thing.... The blue of this blind seemed to me, not perhaps by its beauty but by its intense vividness, to efface so completely all the colors that had passed before my eyes from the day of my birth up to the moment when I had gulped down the last of my drink and it had begun to take effect, that compared with this blue they were as drab, as null, as the darkness in which he has lived must be in retrospect to a man born blind whom a subsequent operation has at length enabled to see and to distinguish colors.[33]

The passage might lead us to think: there may be something to be said for objectivity, after all. Yet is our hero oblivious to the world here, or is he only making contact with it in an unusual manner? The latter is what we must conclude if we are adopting as our principle of interpretation that, as Heidegger affirms, for any mood there is some "peculiar truth or manifestness that lies in this attunement as in every attunement."[34] When we imagine that moods are a comprehensively distorting influence, we are likely regarding it as an embarrassment that we occupy an affective vantage point at all. And no human point of view is devoid of all determinate characteristics whatsoever. Yet, at the same time, we would regard it as a pity if Marcel were to place greater importance on his enraptured view of the window-blind than on the sunrise that he subsequently witnesses *through* the window, after having slept, and the beauty of which he ornately depicts:

There gathered behind it reserves of light. It brightened; the sky turned to a glowing pink which I strove, gluing my eyes to the window, to see more clearly, for I felt that it was related somehow to the most intimate life of Nature, but, the course of the line altering, the train turned, the morning scene gave place in the

---

[33] *Within a Budding Grove*, I: 702.
[34] Heidegger, *Fundamental Concepts of Metaphysics*, 139.

frame of the window to a nocturnal village, its roofs still blue with moonlight, its pond encrusted with the opalescent sheen of night, ... and I was lamenting the loss of my strip of pink sky when I caught sight of it anew, but red this time, in the opposite window which it left at a second bend in the line; so that I spent my time running from one window to the other.[35]

In short, we ought to keep in mind that all our perception, including our emotional perception, is a way of seeing from somewhere—and in some way. To speculate about what things are like *entirely* apart from "interpretation and subjectivity" is, as Nietzsche says, to entertain "a quite idle hypothesis."[36] And if we were to aspire toward the ideal of the universe's own impersonal perspective, "from which all is seen but nothing is cared for,"[37] we would be dead to the meaning of things, lacking the focus and orientation that are required for the conduct of life and the pursuit of knowledge. The reason why it is a pity to be "stuck" in a depressive mood, or one of irascibility or of sentimental nostalgia, or of being awestruck by the brilliant color of the window-blind, is that the way the world seems to us when we are depressed, or irascible, or in one of these other states, is not the *only* way it is. The window-blind contemplator is out of touch with much that is worthy of his attention, as is the nostalgic sentimentalist. What is needed by any of us is the ability to inhabit a diversity of moods, affective standpoints, and perspectives,[38] and not to close our minds to what an atypical

---

[35] *Within a Budding Grove*, I: 704.

[36] Friedrich Nietzsche, *The Will to Power*, ed. Walter Kaufmann (New York: Vintage Books, 1968), § 560. "The beloved contains possible worlds," Deleuze remarks, which can only unfold and be validated in the lover's eyes: *Proust and Signs*, 138.

[37] Margaret Olivia Little, "Seeing and Caring: The Role of Affect in Feminist Epistemology," *Hypatia* 10, no. 3 (1995): 117–137, 125.

[38] For examples of how both Thoreau and Nietzsche describe this capacity and its importance, see Furtak, *Knowing Emotions*, 172–173. On the topic in more general terms see Colombetti, *The Feeling Body*, 77–80. With regard to the physiological basis of a particular mood, see Paul Redding, *The Logic of Affect* (Ithaca, NY: Cornell University Press, 1999), 158: "Reason must navigate on a sea of biological and other natural forces that do

mood might be able to reveal. Even when our infra-red vision is functioning oddly for straightforwardly physical reasons, we still do not find ourselves in a self-enclosed realm, but with an angle of interpretation on the world.

The manner in which we are attuned to our surroundings, the mood that we embody at any given time, invariably opens us toward what is not ourselves and conditions how it seems. To be affectively disposed in some way or other is to sense how things are going in our world of concern, and to have an idea of what is real and significant. That is what a mood can disclose, which is why it is far from being objectless or lacking intentional world-directedness altogether. Possibilities are by their very nature uncertain: nevertheless, they are not for this reason to be dismissed as somehow artificial. In "Proustian reality," as Levinas affirms, evidently "all is dizzyingly possible."[39] And our somatic, affective experience attests to the meaning of our encounters with what is other than us—to how, in the words of one contemporary phenomenologist, "we bear witness to that which has moved us."[40] Each person's attunement is both outwardly and inwardly truth-revealing, because it brings to light aspects of the environment (what we love) while also showing who we are at heart (our way of loving). Proust's narrator is on a search for truth, with the goal of understanding the varieties of truth that are at stake in our lover's quarrel with a so-called "external" world.[41]

not belong to it, but without which it could go nowhere. Affect is our most immediate awareness of the fact that we sail on such a sea."

[39] Levinas, *Proper Names*, 101.
[40] David Michael Levin, *The Body's Recollection of Being: Phenomenological Psychology and the Deconstruction of Nihilism* (London: Routledge and Kegan Paul, 1985), 103. See also page 95, on why authentically becoming oneself is "an *individual* realization of the universal relatedness-to-Being which defines every one of us in a primordial way." Speaking of *sedimentation*, Simone de Beauvoir observes, "she will always trail this past behind her." See *The Second Sex*, trans. Constance Borde and Sheila Malovany-Chevalier (New York: Vintage Books, 2011), 761. On emotions as "Janus-faced," by virtue of being outwardly and inwardly revelatory of (respectively) world and self, see Ronald de Sousa, *Emotional Truth* (New York: Oxford University Press, 2011), 69–70.
[41] In love, Merleau-Ponty notes, "as the other, the true dawns through an emotional and almost carnal experience," not so much "understood" as it is "welcomed or spurned."

38 LOVE, SUBJECTIVITY, AND TRUTH

To learn from it we must avoid throwing out the baby with the bath water: for if we were to reject the potential truthfulness of moods due to the ridiculousness of Marcel's enraptured state of mind in apprehending the window-blind, we would be unable to appreciate the profundity of his attunement when he spends hundreds of pages in *The Fugitive* spelling out how it feels to recognize too late the extent of one's love for a person whom one has irretrievably lost. Yet we have barely begun to enumerate his reasons for being skeptical of how things appear through his infra-red vision.

The Visible and the Invisible, trans. Alphonso Lingis (Evanston, IL: Northwestern University Press, 1968), 12. Regarding how Marcel enacts "in his own body the general human quest for knowledge," see Malcolm Bowie, *Freud, Proust and Lacan: Theory as Fiction* (Cambridge: Cambridge University Press, 1987), 50–51.

3

Skepticism and Perspective

The Elusiveness of Truth

A major conundrum that faces Proust's narrator throughout the novel is whether love puts us in touch with the world or encloses us in a fantasy realm that is of our own making. He subscribes "at least some of the time," as one commentator has noted, "to the theoretical belief that the objectivity of the external world is an illusion."[1] An early recognition Marcel makes regarding Albertine is that, even as he "thought about her endlessly," his imagination had "superimposed upon her being" much that was "of [his] own invention," to the point that his own contribution to her perceived nature outweighs the impressions imposed upon him "from the beloved object" herself.[2] Looking back at the people he has loved, he is astonished that "when I saw them, when I heard their voices, I could find nothing in them which resembled my love and could account for it." He must have "artificially attached" to them fabricated virtues that acquired a "quasi-electric power" over him, like "occult forces."[3] Yet he is relentlessly driven to *know* what he loves, to comprehend what it is about the beloved—and what about himself—that can explain his enchantment. The epistemic concerns of Proust's novel derive from the way that Marcel "hears, and heeds,

---

[1] Jones, *Philosophy and the Novel*, 148–151 and 158.
[2] *Within a Budding Grove*, I: 917–918.
[3] *Cities of the Plain*, II: 1164–1165. Marcel's view as articulated here is that "the feeling of love has nothing to do with the emotion we can derive from the beauty, the intelligence or the kindness of the one we love." See also de Beistegui, *Proust as Philosopher: The Art of Metaphor*, 8–9: "The real significance of love . . . is epistemological."

an imperious call to *know*," which weaves into the fabric of his text "one of the most elaborate and circumstantial portrayals of the theorizing mind that European culture possesses."[4] According to one of his later formulations, his quest is to capture and understand the impressions that have "been dictated to us by reality," that have "been printed in us by reality itself."[5] He is the *zetetic* type of skeptic, who keeps on searching for the truth, convinced that it is there to be found.

It seems that at least intermittently Marcel believes that it *is* possible to achieve some knowledge of the outside world, in particular the minds of others whom we love. "Love is directed at the *partially* knowable reality of another," or so he gives us reason to think.[6] As keenly aware as he is of the obstacles to emotional knowledge, Marcel nonetheless keeps reflecting on how it *may* be attainable to a degree. His obsessive inquiry is unquestionably central to *In Search of Lost Time*, and at the heart of my own project here is the attempt to figure out what sort of truth might be available through the subjectivity of a loving person. Accordingly, I shall present a systematic inventory of Marcel's more and less skeptical opinions; the organizing principle that I employ is the set of classical Pyrrhonian modes of suspending judgment, of which there are ten. Sextus Empiricus attests that they are listed in no particular sequence.[7]

---

[4] Bowie, *Freud, Proust and Lacan: Theory as Fiction*, 49 and 65. See also Alexander Nehamas, "Only in the Contemplation of Beauty is Human Life Worth Living," *European Journal of Philosophy* 15 (2007): 1–18: "To love something is always, in part, to try to understand what makes it beautiful, what drew me and, as long as I still love it, continues to draw me toward it" (8). Cf. Alexander Nehamas, *Only a Promise of Happiness* (Princeton, NJ: Princeton University Press, 2007), 131.

[5] *Time Regained*, III: 914. Regarding what follows, viz. the "zetetic" school of Hellenistic skepticism, see Sextus Empiricus, *Outlines of Pyrrhonism*, 1.7. Unless otherwise indicated, all translations from this text are by R. G. Bury (Amherst, NY: Prometheus Books, 1990).

[6] Kubala, "Love and Transience in Proust," 542–543. My emphasis.

[7] See Sextus Empiricus, *Outlines of Pyrrhonism*, 1.36–1.163. See also *The Hellenistic Philosophers, Volume One*, trans. A. A. Long and D. N. Sedley (Cambridge: Cambridge University Press, 1987), 473–488. On Marcel's skepticism, see Nussbaum, *Love's Knowledge*, 265–274, esp. 271: "He wishes not to be tormented by the ungovernable inner life" of Albertine, so he becomes "skeptical" about whether her inner life is real.

Some of these categories may overlap, yet overall they serve well as an organizing principle.

i.

The world, as Husserl points out, "is dubitable not in the sense that rational motives are present" which suffice to prevail over "the tremendous force of harmonious experiences," but "rather in the sense that a doubt is *conceivable*"; and it *is*, for "the whole *spatiotemporal world*" has "intentional being," or "being *for* a consciousness."[8] As Wittgenstein asserts in his compact manner, "What solipsism *means* is quite correct," namely "that the world is *my* world."[9] Human existence is, in each case, one's own, in other words—the way things appear is always how they appear to *someone*. From this observation is born the first skeptical argument in favor of suspending judgment: the way that "the same impressions are not produced by the same objects," by virtue of the "differences" among creatures.[10] It is striking that among the first examples used by Sextus Empiricus to illustrate this claim is a Proustian one, so to speak: "if we bend down over a book after having gazed long and fixedly at the sun, the letters seem to us to be golden in color and circling round."[11] We might recall that when Marcel gets intoxicated on the train and attempts to read, the words apparently do something like swirl around on the page, and he cannot focus on them. He also describes sitting at an earlier stage of life under the shade of a sun-shielded garden chair in Combray, gazing so fixedly

---

[8] Edmund Husserl, *Ideas Pertaining to a Pure Phenomenology and to a Phenomenological Philosophy, First Book*, trans. Fred Kersten (The Hague: Martinus Nijhoff Publishers, 1982), 103–112.

[9] Ludwig Wittgenstein, *Tractatus Logico-Philosophicus*, trans. C. K. Ogden (London: Routledge & Kegan Paul, 1955), 5.62.

[10] Sextus Empiricus, *Outlines of Pyrrhonism*, 1.40. To highlight the continuity between ancient and modern forms of skeptical doubt, I will always use a lowercase *s* when referring to "skepticism."

[11] Sextus Empiricus, *Outlines of Pyrrhonism*, 1.45.

upon the book he was reading that afternoon that he was scarcely conscious of the hours striking from the steeple of a nearby church. "Sometimes," he would hear it "sound two strokes more than the last," showing that there had been "an hour which I had not heard strike," that "something that had taken place had not taken place for me."[12] This disconcerting discrepancy between the objective world and his subjective experience of it prompts one of his earliest musings about being and seeming. In short, what reality could an audi*ble* noise have, if it sounded but was unheard? And what else might Marcel be failing to apprehend?

The metaphysical plot thickens when we turn our attention to the differences among living creatures that Sextus has more obviously in mind. When Robert de Saint-Loup's mistress moves into a little house near Versailles with her dogs, monkey, canaries, and parakeet, she has with her various kinds of ears and eyes,[13] with varying capacities for receiving sensory impressions. Some of her pets can hear sounds that do not even *exist* for a human being. Where we find a perspective, we find a subject who "construes all the rest of the world from its own viewpoint," or in its particular manner.[14] This thought brings us back to a passage I cited earlier:

> I realized that it is not only the physical world that differs from the aspect in which we see it; that all reality is perhaps equally dissimilar . . . just as the trees, the sun and the sky would not be the same as what we see if they were apprehended by creatures having eyes differently constituted from ours, or else endowed for that purpose with organs other than eyes which would furnish equivalents of trees and sky and sun, though not visual ones.[15]

---

[12] *Swann's Way*, I: 94.

[13] See *The Guermantes Way*, II: 123. By an earlier tally, her pets include one dog, multiple canaries, and many parrots: see *Within a Budding Grove*, I: 839.

[14] Nietzsche, *The Will to Power*, § 636. Or, in the words of Thomas Nagel, for any conscious organism "there is something it is like to *be* that organism," although as for its experience "the form may vary." See "What Is It Like to Be a Bat?," in *Mortal Questions* (Cambridge: Cambridge University Press, 1979), 165–180, 166.

[15] *The Guermantes Way*, II: 64.

Notice how nearly this resembles the following excerpt from a concise account of how the world as we apprehend it is dependent on our mental faculties: "What we can perceive, experience, or know must inevitably depend not only on what there is to perceive, experience, or know but also on whatever apparatus we have for perceiving, experiencing, and knowing."[16] Extend this general claim to our affective life, and we find another kind of divergence between one perspective and another. How can it be that Rachel and Albertine each appear so different to Robert and to Marcel?[17] The two men's vantage points regarding what is significant and worthy of attention diverge as greatly as do those of the philosopher and his pet in a famous example:

> Take our dogs and ourselves, connected as we are by a tie more intimate than most ties in this world; and yet, outside of that tie of friendly fondness, how insensible, each of us, to all that makes life significant for the other—we to the rapture of bones under hedges, or smells of trees and lamp-posts, they to the delights of literature and art. As you sit reading the most moving romance you ever fell upon, what sort of a judge is your fox-terrier of your behavior? With all his goodwill toward you, the nature of your conduct is absolutely excluded from his comprehension. To sit there like a senseless statue, when you might be taking him to walk and throwing sticks for him to catch! What queer disease is this that comes over you every day, of holding things and staring at them like that for hours together, paralyzed of motion and vacant of all conscious life?[18]

---

[16] Bryan Magee, *The Philosophy of Schopenhauer* (Oxford: Clarendon Press, 1983), 64. As Magee points out on page 74, this means that "our perceptions and conceptions cannot be all there is, but cannot be 'like' what exists in addition to them" either.

[17] See, e.g., *The Guermantes Way*, II: 160–164 and 233–234.

[18] William James, "On a Certain Blindness in Human Beings," in *Selected Writings*, ed. G. H. Bird (London: Everyman, 1995), 320–337, 320–321.

This "blindness with which we are all afflicted" with respect to "the feelings of creatures and people different from ourselves," as William James calls it, is not only evident in a case such as this. Proust's novel repeatedly attests that there are many kinds of blindness.

When Albertine and her friends make their first appearance, like "a flock of gulls" along the shore, what strikes Marcel is how *unknown* is the viewpoint that each of them embodies.[19] This feminine "assembly of birds," distinctive and unique in every case, harbors a concealed point of view behind each pair of eyes that would occasionally alight upon him, looking out from within "an inaccessible, unknown world."[20] Of Albertine, he asks himself: "From the depths of what universe did she discern me?" And he remarks that, "if we thought that the eyes of such a girl were merely two glittering sequins of mica, we should not be athirst to know her." As it is, however, he longs to gain access to her subjective outlook—to "what was in her eyes"—to bring this closer and make it into part of his world. That, at least, is one way to interpret what it means to make the beloved one's own.[21] It is, as Marcel has believed ever since his first encounter with Gilberte, to infiltrate "the unknown world of her existence," in this case to gain a view into Albertine's "ideas" and "plans," along with "her desires, her sympathies, her revulsions," as well as "the people and places she knows"—in short, her entire affective sensibility, everything that distinguishes her perspective and mode of being—even if this woman, as a separate creature, must always remain partially unknown to him.

---

[19] *Within a Budding Grove*, I: 845–847. On "the psychologically fatal step from the general to the particular" taken by Proust's narrator, see Henry Sussman, *The Hegelian Aftermath* (Baltimore: Johns Hopkins University Press, 1982), 213–214.

[20] *Within a Budding Grove*, I: 850–853. The rest of the passages I cite in this paragraph are from these pages as well, unless otherwise noted.

[21] Cf. Nehamas, "Only in the Contemplation of Beauty is Human Life Worth Living," 7–9; see also Nehamas, *Only a Promise of Happiness*, 55. As for Marcel's initial wish to gain entrance to Gilberte's "unknown world," see *Swann's Way*, I: 154–155.

Again, we see how the reasons for what I above portrayed as the epistemic concerns of the novel, as well as its preoccupation with all the various grounds for skeptical doubt, are linked with the prospect of what might be called *emotional knowing* in all its forms. Swann, through his love for Odette, finds that the "passion for truth" he had known in younger years is reviving, as his curiosity about her brings to life "the same thirst for knowledge with which he had once studied history."[22] Likewise, Marcel has his longing to know awakened in his relationship with Albertine most of all, and will by turns represent himself as pursuing many different kinds of scientific research in the service of his overriding epistemological imperative. Just as ancient skeptics wondered at those facets of the world unavailable to us that must be routinely included in the perceptions of other animals,[23] the protagonist marvels at everything that is hidden in Albertine's mind. "The belief that a person has a share in an unknown life" is, "of all the prerequisites of love, the one which it values most highly,"[24] yet this unknown existence is not the sort of thing that can be known with scientific certainty. To love is therefore an infinite task.

The characteristically human "attraction to an acutely different existence," in the life of a non-human animal or in the alterity of a different human being than oneself,[25] is understood in Proust's novel as a yearning to gain access to their unobtainable existence. In *The Captive*, Albertine's subjectivity is depicted in a series of metaphors that suggest greater and greater degrees of opacity. She is first a cat, then a plant, then a stone, whose inner core is as inaccessible from without as the contents of a sealed envelope.[26] Marcel

---

[22] *Swann's Way*, I: 298–299. Regarding what follows, see also Bowie, *Freud, Proust and Lacan: Theory as Fiction*, 50.

[23] On the dog, for instance, and its keen senses of smell and hearing, see Sextus Empiricus, *Outlines of Pyrrhonism*, 1.64.

[24] *Swann's Way*, I: 108.

[25] Edward J. Hughes, *Marcel Proust: A Study in the Quality of Awareness* (Cambridge: Cambridge University Press, 1983), 20–21.

[26] See, e.g., *The Captive*, III: 6, 64, 71, 89, and 393.

is of the opinion that a person's visible beauty is partially a manifestation of her inwardness, her psyche, her way of life: even those who "claim to judge" others by "looks alone" see in their appearance an "emanation" from within, just as Swann can perceive in Odette's beauty her "soul . . . rising to the surface of her face."[27] Something is *in* the other, which can be partly expressed yet remain largely hidden. In light of this, it is clearly a cop-out on the part of Marcel to describe the beloved as a mere "phantom," whose "reality existed to a great extent in my imagination."[28] We must be cautious toward all the declarations by Proust's narrator to the effect that "truth and beauty are in us, not in the object."[29] These are tentative hypotheses that might be disproven by other moments in the narrative, rather than definitive statements of the author's considered view. Yet it remains the case that the way things appear depends on our particular subjectivity.

ii.

The second skeptical mode of suspending judgment is based on the differences among human beings, by virtue of their "peculiarities" or "idiosyncrasies."[30] Proust's novel is filled with illustrations of how people can be affected by the same things in radically different

---

[27] See *Swann's Way*, I: 108 and 268. This image is expertly enhanced in Milan Kundera's use of the phrase "The crew of her soul rushed to the deck of her body," said of Tereza in *The Unbearable Lightness of Being*, trans. Michael Henry Heim (New York: Perennial Classics, 1999), 41 and 50.

[28] *Cities of the Plain*, II: 1045. Marcel elsewhere implies that imagination is required to appreciate beauty, when he remarks that exceptional beauty can be left "to men with no imagination." See *The Fugitive*, III: 446–447.

[29] John Porter Houston, *The Shape and Style of Proust's Novel* (Detroit: Wayne State University Press, 1982), 16–17. Against this trend, Colin Falck argues that our imagination *can* open us to reality: see *Myth, Truth, and Literature* (Cambridge: Cambridge University Press, 1989), 136–138. Cf. Ong, *The Art of Being*, 185, on how for Sartre the role of imagination in disclosing the world faces constraints; our situation is therefore not "a subjective projection."

[30] Sextus Empiricus, *Outlines of Pyrrhonism*, 1.79ff.

ways, and this is often taken to cast doubt on the nature of whatever object is thus affecting them. Marcel remarks of himself and Saint-Loup that there is "a gulf between the images that he and I respectively had of his mistress,"[31] although as we have seen it would be naïve to conclude that this difference is one in which the narrator simply has an exact view of Rachel and Saint-Loup an inaccurate one. Instead, *each* of the two men is relying upon his own idiosyncratic disposition, so neither can be regarded as authoritative. "No doubt it was the same thin and narrow face that we saw, Robert and I. But we had arrived at it by two opposite ways which would never converge, and we would never both see it from the same side."[32] Nor can either of the two see himself into the other's point of view. A telling reversal takes place later in the novel, when Robert expects a photo of Albertine to reveal her as a stunning and wonderful beauty, and is stupefied to see that she appears so ordinary: how, he asks himself, could the friend he admires have been so powerfully struck by *her*? Saint-Loup has trouble hiding his astonishment, and Marcel recognizes that "the difference between our respective impressions of the same person" was as great as in the earlier case of Rachel.[33] Here, he seems to regard their divergent perspectives as fundamentally irreconcilable, having ceased to give priority to the cynical view *or* the charitable one.

To each mind, there corresponds a different world.[34] The lesson is one that Marcel finds it difficult to learn, as evidenced by his youthful belief that his parents must "experience the same emotions," feeling the same way as he himself does—about his beloved hawthorn blossoms, or about his encounter with Odette at

---

[31] See *The Guermantes Way*, II: 177. See also *The Guermantes Way*, II: 233–234.
[32] *The Guermantes Way*, II: 161. Cf. Nietzsche, *The Gay Science*, § 374.
[33] *The Fugitive*, III: 445–446. On the normative claim made on the one who is moved by a specific response to beauty, see Richard Moran, *The Philosophical Imagination* (Oxford: Oxford University Press, 2017), 84–85.
[34] Cf. Nietzsche, *Thus Spake Zarathustra*, trans. Walter Kaufmann (New York: Penguin Books, 1978), 217: "To every soul there belongs another world."

his Uncle Adolphe's.[35] "I learned that identical emotions do not spring up simultaneously in the hearts of all men in accordance with a pre-established order,"[36] he laments—although he does not cease to formulate theories about what human beings must universally feel based on experiences that are quite peculiar to himself. Idiosyncratically personal, "subjective" truths do not have sweeping applicability: indeed, some of the general maxims about love that are put forward in Proust's novel "apply only to the set of people like Marcel, a set which at times contains but a single member."[37] Yet Marcel's tendency is understandable. After all, none of us wants *our* world to be hopelessly out of touch with *the* world.

The painting by Elstir of the harbor at Carquethuit first makes Marcel think that he would like to see a place so beautiful, but later it occurs to him that the novel character manifested so distinctly in the picture "might belong perhaps rather to the painter's vision than to any special quality in the place itself."[38] By these lights, beauty is either *all* in the object or entirely in the beholder's eye. Opting for the latter explanation, he is frequently content to think that if another person finds something beautiful only due to some subjective feature of his or her composition, then he himself is missing nothing by failing to perceive that supposed beauty. Yet Elstir provokes him to be dissatisfied with this facile conclusion: what if, Marcel cannot help but wonder, the painter's mode of vision allows him, Elstir, to gain access to beautiful sights that others are unable to see? In the case of the Balbec church, when Marcel admits his disappointment upon seeing it for the first time, Elstir is shocked to hear this and gives him an enthusiastic account of its ornate images,

---

[35] *Swann's Way*, I: 157–158. On his response to the mysterious "lady in pink" at his uncle's home, see *Swann's Way*, I: 82–85.
[36] *Swann's Way*, I: 170.
[37] Landy, *Philosophy as Fiction*, 28–32. Cf. Rex Ferguson, "*In Search of Lost Time* and the Attunement of Jealousy," *Philosophy and Literature* 41, no. 1 (2017): 213–232, 215–216. Relatedly, see *Within a Budding Grove*, I: 716–717. On "subjective truth" see *The Captive*, III: 354–355.
[38] *Within a Budding Grove*, I: 894–895 and 913.

forcing our narrator to confess to himself sheepishly that "it was not this vast celestial vision of which he spoke to me that I had seen."[39] The failure was not in the church's artwork, Marcel realizes, but in his own attunement.[40] As Kierkegaard has written, "all observation is not just a receiving, a discovering, but also a bringing forth, and insofar as it is that, how the observer himself is constituted is indeed decisive."[41] Elstir, like any other artist, offers a way of seeing, depicting things from a determinate perspective. However, although *what* one sees decisively depends upon *how* one sees, a role can still be played by what is there to be seen. It seems that Marcel should not neglect the importance of the outside world *or* of each person's orientation toward it.

In his ongoing effort to work out "an erotics of truth," Proust's "epistemophiliac narrator" is liable to be tormented when he reflects upon how another person's view must reveal things that he is unable to perceive.[42] Because Marcel, unlike his creator, is a heterosexual male, it is with the eyes of one that he gazes on Albertine's mackintosh, or the wetness that makes it seem to be clinging to her body as though to take her imprint for a sculptor. Yet the beauty of her very form, he realizes, must be different—in ways that he *knows* he cannot imagine—from the standpoint of a *woman* who also finds Albertine attractive.[43] His obsession with her postulated lesbian lovers (and desires) derives much of its intensity from the

---

[39] *Within a Budding Grove*, I: 899–901.

[40] The classical source of the idea that, to see beauty, a person must have a certain type of attunement, is Plotinus, *Enneads*, 1.6. The existential *locus classicus*, meanwhile, is probably Heidegger, *Being and Time*, § 29.

[41] Søren Kierkegaard, *Eighteen Upbuilding Discourses*, trans. Howard V. Hong and Edna H. Hong (Princeton, NJ: Princeton University Press, 1990), 59. Cf. Rawlinson, "Art and Truth: Reading Proust," 12. See also Nishida Kitarō's *An Inquiry into the Good*, trans. Masao Abe and Christopher Ives (New Haven, CT: Yale University Press, 1990), 134: "From a certain angle, the objective world of each individual is a reflection of his or her personality." We may also be reminded here of Scheler on the correlation between person and world, for instance in *Formalism in Ethics and Non-Formal Ethics of Values*, 395.

[42] Duncan Large, *Nietzsche and Proust: A Comparative Study* (Oxford: Clarendon Press, 2001), 136–137. Italics removed.

[43] See *Cities of the Plain*, II: 894 and 1157–1158. Cf. *The Captive*, III: 392.

fact that their feelings are beyond the realm of what he can conceive of. All too seldom, until quite late in the novel, are the moments when Marcel finds beauty in having his own finite perspective, rather than regarding his finitude as a deplorable kind of confinement: that, for instance, Albertine's body contains for him (and not for any other lover, of whatever description) the traces of all those days the two of them have spent together in Balbec,[44] such that her presence in Paris brings with it a palpable sense of the sea coast and the prior summer. In this sense, then, their shared history *constitutes* his access to the world, rather than constraining it. As we might expect, though, the skeptic in Marcel tends to think of the differences among human beings as affording mainly grounds for doubt.

He therefore wonders if, just as people ascribe a meaning (for example) to New Year's Day, which "the blind laws of nature" cannot be expected to recognize,[45] perhaps a person who loves is also guilty of falsifying things. He continually reverts to associating love with merely subjective feelings, which assign to the beloved "what exists only in the person who loves," stretching "to its maximum the distance between objective reality and love." Yet he never remains satisfied with this theoretical stance for very long. "The subjective element" in vision, he writes within a few pages, does not "make reality vanish into pure relativism."[46] He appreciates that it is painful for Swann to be surrounded by people who regard his love as "a subjective state which existed for himself alone," as they are plainly out of touch with major contours of the reality that Swann inhabits.[47] Marcel is not convinced that, in such differences of opinion, it must always be the lover who is deluded: he rejects the type of "subjective

---

[44] *The Guermantes Way*, II: 363. On our sense of epistemic "confinement" due to the a priori limits of possible experience, see Stanley Cavell, *Pursuits of Happiness* (Cambridge, MA: Harvard University Press, 1981), 77–78.
[45] *Within a Budding Grove*, I: 525–526.
[46] See *Time Regained*, III: 950–951 and 952.
[47] *Swann's Way*, I: 375. Scheler would say that this only demonstrates that all the "blindness" is "on the side of the 'detached observer.'" *The Nature of Sympathy*, 160.

idealism" that turns reality into the subject's creation,[48] along with the notion often ascribed to him, that love subsists on illusion. Not decidedly giving priority to blindness over infra-red vision, Marcel confesses that he is unsure of whether Rachel "the tart" is any "more real" than the enchanting Rachel whom Saint-Loup loves.[49] Evidently, the concept of objective reality does not get eliminated from consideration.

At one point when he is trying to adjust his lenses, he conceives of a mechanism that would be able to take truly unbiased measurements, leaving the observer along with his or her "incessant love" out of the equation, and recording the action as "a photographic plate" that has no need, somehow, of itself requiring to be interpreted.[50] Yet a pure, emotionless view that could deliver an observer-free observation is as futile an aim as Marcel's related conjecture of a mathematical average that could be located between the extremes of fervent love and utter indifference. It is rather ludicrous when the incompatibility between Gilberte's significance "in my eyes" and what she is "in the eyes of other people" leads him to fantasize about identifying "between these two perspectives, equally distorting, a third which would enable me to see things as they really were."[51] Here, the imaginary remedy for the "distortions" of a lover's heightened attention and the outlook of a detached bystander is to find a halfway place between the two. Yet the fact that Gilberte at the time looms big in Marcel's world, while having miniscule significance in the eyes of indifferent onlookers, does not imply that her "real" importance is midway in between—or best seen through a pair of glasses that Kierkegaard speculates about, with one lens

[48] As Sartrean existentialism is described, and opposed to the Proustian view, by Genevieve Lloyd in *Being in Time: Selves and Narrators in Philosophy and Literature* (London: Routledge, 1993), 132–133.
[49] See *The Guermantes Way*, II: 164–165. See also Descombes, *Proust: Philosophy of the Novel*, 27: in Proust's terminology, "the existence of the external world" denotes "the role played in the birth of love by the reality of the person loved."
[50] *The Guermantes Way*, II: 142. Kierkegaard comments on how the "same" facts will seem quite different to a person who loves: see *Works of Love*, 227–228.
[51] *Within a Budding Grove*, I: 631.

52 LOVE, SUBJECTIVITY, AND TRUTH

that magnifies immensely while the other reduces just as much.[52] When we cannot grasp how life appears to another person, this is not a quantitative difference—not a matter of simply wanting *more* of something to which we already have access to an extent.

Sextus Empiricus is fond of illustrations dealing with radical differences in our faculties of sensory perception, for instance, the butler who reputedly "used to shiver when he was in the sun or in a hot bath, but felt warm in the shade."[53] And, while Proust's narrator does comment on the curious phenomenon of enjoying a cold bath, what most nearly matches Sextus's example is an episode involving Marcel's grandmother and the sea breeze at Balbec. Bathilde, not wanting to have the wind blocked out by the glass windows in the dining room of the Grand Hotel where she and her grandson were having lunch,

> surreptitiously opened a pane and at once sent flying, together with the menus, the newspapers, veils and hats of all the people at the other tables, while she herself, fortified by the celestial draught, remained calm and smiling like Saint Blandina amid the torrent of invective which . . . those contemptuous, disheveled, furious visitors combined to pour on us.[54]

If we think she is wrong to find the wind invigorating and delightful, what is our justification for this? That she is outnumbered, perhaps? But surely, as a classical skeptic would tell us, this cannot settle the matter. Or that the breeze also has the capability of upsetting newspapers and hats? That is equally well regarded with a sense of

---

[52] Kierkegaard, *Papers and Journals*, 95 (*Papirer* II A 203; *KJN* DD: 90).
[53] Sextus Empiricus, *Outlines of Pyrrhonism*, 1.82. On cold baths, see *The Captive*, III: 184.
[54] *Within a Budding Grove*, I: 725–726. As for the flawed ideal of appealing to a majority vote, see Sextus Empiricus, *Outlines of Pyrrhonism*, 1.89. The view that truth is whatever people deem it to be is rebuked in Kierkegaard's work, since what matters "is truth for you." *Either/Or*, trans. Alastair Hannay (New York: Penguin Books, 1992), 51 and 609.

humor, as an amusing farce. The same phenomena affect us in different ways, and when they do it is by no means always clear that one person is mistaken while the other is correct.

More troubling for Proust's characters is the way that any of us can be different beings in sequence, especially as we go through the births and deaths of our loves. Charles Swann learns to appreciate in Odette features that did not initially seem captivating to him,[55] and his love for her grows until it reaches the point where, as physicians say, it "was no longer operable,"[56] so deeply was it entrenched in his heart. Yet "the heart changes, and it is our worst sorrow,"[57] as Swann himself learns when, after much damage has been done, he begins to feel that his love is diminishing:

> In the past, having often thought with terror that a day must come when he would cease to be in love with Odette, he had determined to keep a sharp look-out, and as soon as he felt that love was beginning to leave him, to cling to it and hold it back. But now, to the diminution of his love there corresponded a simultaneous diminution in his desire to remain in love. For a man cannot change, that is to say become another person, while continuing to obey the dictates of the self which he has ceased to be.[58]

Marcel, who likewise becomes another person after surviving the death of the self that loved Gilberte, then yet another after suffering the death of the self that loved Albertine, reflects that "the truth is so variable for each of us" that it is difficult for anyone, oneself or another, to know what it is.[59] Finding a fixed, unchanging standpoint is out of the question in matters of the heart.

---

[55] See, e.g., *Swann's Way*, I: 213 and 269. That she "wasn't even my type," as he keeps saying—see *Swann's Way*, I: 415—is true of his *first* impression, and part of the tragedy of his eventual love for her.

[56] *Swann's Way*, I: 336.

[57] *Swann's Way*, I: 92.

[58] *Swann's Way*, I: 410.

[59] *The Captive*, III: 11–12. This observation is located between the death of the self who loved Gilberte and the death of the self who loved Albertine: on Gilberte, see *Within*

When the narrator loves Albertine, it is of the utmost importance to distinguish her voice from those of the other young women, and to perceive where exactly her beauty mark is located.[60] Once he no longer loves her, Albertine's singularity dissolves into the undifferentiated background, as part of an anonymous mass. This change conflicts with his wish for love to seem "absolutely necessary and predestined,"[61] because it suggests that accidents of circumstance are enormously influential on how the world is disclosed to each of us. Thus, another difference due to idiosyncrasy that may give rise to skepticism is that between the person we have become and the countless variants of ourselves that we might have been—if only this or that contingency had been other than it was. It vexes Marcel to no end that his love "may spring up again in the future," that it "could have sprung up already in the past, for another person," and that someone "who has thus determined the course of our life has, in so doing, excluded all the lives which we might have led instead of our actual life."[62] Had it not been that Swann "had inspired in me the wish to go to Balbec, where otherwise my parents would never have had the idea of sending me," Marcel reflects, then "I should never have known Albertine."[63] Proust's narrator *could* view the fortuities that allowed this love to come into being as the sort of blessings that only chance can bestow, yet more often what is it that happens? As Merleau-Ponty notes, the "elements of contingency or of chance" in a love tend to "make us *doubt* love."[64]

---

a Budding Grove, I: 691 and *Cities of the Plain*, II: 739; on Albertine, see *The Fugitive*, III: 657–659 and *Time Regained*, III: 1094–1095.

[60] The mole that Marcel thought he might have seen on her cheek or chin "came to rest for ever on her upper lip": see *Within a Budding Grove*, I: 938. And, as for how "loving helps us to discern, to discriminate," e.g., the voice of the beloved, see *Within a Budding Grove*, I: 969. On how "the end of love is like a return to the initial indivisibility of the *jeunes filles*," see Gilles Deleuze, *Proust and Signs*, 176.
[61] *The Guermantes Way*, II: 408. See also Kubala, "Love and Transience in Proust," 554.
[62] See *The Guermantes Way*, II: 658; then, *Time Regained*, III: 955.
[63] *Time Regained*, III: 953–954. Cf. *The Fugitive*, III: 510–511.
[64] Maurice Merleau-Ponty, *Institution and Passivity*, trans. Leonard Lawlor and Heath Massey (Evanston, IL: Northwestern University Press, 2010), 29–33. On love's contingencies, see Kundera, *The Unbearable Lightness of Being*, 49.

iii.

The same phenomenologist of embodiment maintains that "the unity of the object will remain a mystery for us as long as we think of its various qualities (its color and taste, for example) as just so many data belonging to the entirely distinct worlds of sight, smell, touch, and so on." Rather, a thing's "affective meaning" is "reaffirmed" by "each of its qualities," in such a way that a painting should contain, as it were, "even the smell of the landscape."[65] Yet again, an ancient skeptic would find in the disclosures of different senses grounds for suspending judgment about how things actually are:[66] a painting depicts to the eye a scene with "recesses and projections" that touch cannot discern; honey and perfume are respectively pleasing to our senses of taste and smell, whereas neither seems sweet when applied to the eyes. A contemporary scholar of Pyrrhonian skepticism, instead of suspending judgment, offers the dogmatic verdict that, in reality, perfume and gold have "no intrinsic value,"[67] indeed *no* qualities of their own at all.

However, the cold comforts provided by such a nihilistic theory of value fail to account for Marcel's potently ambivalent experience when, for instance, he finds Albertine bitter and sweet, like a poison and its remedy that both originate from the same source;[68] or when it seems that, before his eyes, she flits between seeming "beautiful" and "drab," the latter when she lacks an aura of mystery.[69] In these cases he is inclined to wonder: what *is* she like? Which of his impressions, in other words, can be relied upon to reveal the truth? This problem is complicated by the shifts that Proust's narrator

---

[65] Maurice Merleau-Ponty, *The World of Perception*, trans. Oliver Davis (London and New York: Routledge, 2004), 59–62; *Phenomenology of Perception*, 371.
[66] Sextus Empiricus, *Outlines of Pyrrhonism*, 1.92–93.
[67] See R. J. Hankinson, *The Sceptics* (New York: Routledge, 1995), 168–176.
[68] *Cities of the Plain*, II: 1156. On the *pharmakon* as affliction and cure, see Jacques Derrida's account in *Dissemination*, trans. Barbara Johnson (Chicago: University of Chicago Press, 1981), 95–117.
[69] *The Captive*, III: 170–171.

undergoes in his own manner of being interested. It is not that his perspectival world is a "world for the eye, tongue, and ear," as if these sensory modes of apprehension can only disclose something "very false," as Nietzsche suggests at one point, but that—to extend a Nietzschean theme—the strength and nature of our *interest* in knowing influence what appears to us,[70] as Marcel exemplifies in relation to his beloved. Aware that "moral uncertainty is a greater obstacle to an exact visual perception than any defect of vision would be," and that doubt about what another person feels can affect how we see her,[71] he recognizes that Albertine may appear sweeter or more bitter in light of how *he* is disposed, as much as owing to her own state.

The somatic nature of our affective life can lead to such curious sensory confusions as when "to feel cold" means "not that one ought to warm oneself but that, for instance, one has received a scolding,"[72] or when in torrid weather "sensual desire" moves one not to long for "the kiss of a girl" but for a cool drink.[73] It takes nothing away from the sweetness of orangeade, though, that our access to this quality is via the perceptual modality of taste, rather than that of sound. If any sensory faculty or way of being attuned reveals certain qualities and not others, this is perhaps best accounted for by accepting that every attunement brings to light *some* aspect of the truth. Only to a person whose senses were "seriously deranged" would "the sight of a color" feel "like an incision in his living flesh," so we rightly disregard this case as an exception to the general rule.[74] Proust's narrator does not complain that a painter communicates his or her unique

---

[70] Nietzsche, *The Will to Power*, §§ 602 and 588 respectively. See also Poellner, "Perspectival Truth," in *Nietzsche*, ed. Richardson and Leiter, 98–100.

[71] *The Captive*, III: 135–136. Cf. Merleau-Ponty, *Phenomenology of Perception*, 436, on how a doubt about the object viewed "attaches to vision itself." He rejects the Cartesian conflation of sight with a *presumption*, seeming to see.

[72] Proust, *Within a Budding Grove*, I: 534.

[73] *Cities of the Plain*, II: 669.

[74] *The Captive*, III: 254.

idea of the world in visible form, whereas a composer expresses it through music: each artist presents us with nothing less than a *world* complete unto itself, through a particular faculty.[75] Vinteuil is not depriving his listeners by giving *only* musical embodiment to "the mode by which he 'heard' the universe," for this acquaints us with "a unique world" that no one else could have revealed.[76] And maybe "a universe that was exclusively audible might be as full of variety" as any other,[77] or so Marcel invites us to consider. If he finds himself bemoaning how hard it is to determine what is true, this is not because of any conflicts in the evidence given by different modes of perception.

A dish of exotic food might look unpalatable at first glance, yet taste delicious when we try it, and we are free to give our assent to the latter impression.[78] But another reason for suspending judgment—based on a more profound type of concern—is also included within the third Pyrrhonian mode. This one is not easy to overcome: speaking of an apple, Sextus points out that "the apple may possibly possess more qualities than those apparent to us." He continues:

> Let us imagine a man who possesses from birth the senses of touch, taste, and smell, but [who] can neither hear nor see. This man, then, will assume that nothing visual or audible has any existence, but only those three kinds of qualities which he is able to apprehend. Possibly, then, we also, having only our five senses, perceive only such of the apple's qualities as we are capable of

---

[75] See *Time Regained*, III: 932. See also Descombes, *Proust: Philosophy of the Novel*, 51: every "subjectivity" is "a partiality of the senses."
[76] *The Captive*, III: 382. Cf. Vladimir Jankélévitch, *Music and the Ineffable*, trans. Carolyn Abbate (Princeton, NJ: Princeton University Press, 2003), 12: "Why should hearing, alone among all the senses, have the privilege of accessing the 'thing in itself' for us, and thus destroy the limits of our finitude?"
[77] *The Captive*, III: 78.
[78] Cf. Paul Woodruff, "The Pyrrhonian Modes," in *The Cambridge Companion to Ancient Scepticism*, ed. Richard Bett (Cambridge: Cambridge University Press, 2010), 208–231, 219–220.

apprehending; and possibly it may possess other underlying qualities which affect other sense organs, though we, not being endowed with those organs, fail to apprehend the sense objects which come through them.[79]

This brings to mind the passage in Proust that envisions creatures endowed "with organs other than eyes which would furnish equivalents of trees and sky and sun, though not visual ones."[80] For example, a bat's capacity for echolocation enables it to perceive in such a way that its experiences have "a specific subjective character" which is, nevertheless, "beyond our ability to conceive."[81] In other words, the problem is not that our senses are deceptive or conflicting, but that we are limited *to* what our senses *can* reveal. And the boundaries of the human mind are not the boundaries of reality, so it is reasonable to accept the skeptical claim. Regardless of whether we believe that another being's subjective outlook incorporates a perceptual apparatus involving faculties utterly beyond our own, or simply that other kinds of interpersonal difference render us unintelligible to one another, either way we may justly invoke the concept of the "noumenal" when we refer to the inaccessibility of another person's mind;[82] Schopenhauer points out that "everyone knows *himself* directly, but everything else only very indirectly. This is the fact and the problem."

---

[79] Sextus Empiricus, *Outlines of Pyrrhonism*, 1.96–97. Cf. Magee, *The Philosophy of Schopenhauer*, 57–58.

[80] Again, see *The Guermantes Way*, II: 64. See also *The Fugitive*, III: 699.

[81] Nagel, "What is it Like to Be a Bat?," 169–170. He adds that "the problem is not confined to exotic cases, however, for it exists between one person and another," offering exactly the same example that Sextus Empiricus uses.

[82] As, for instance, John Porter Houston does: see *The Shape and Style of Proust's Novel*, 12–14 and 54. The passage that follows is from Schopenhauer, *The World as Will and Representation, Volume Two*, trans. Judith Norman, Alistair Welchman, and Christopher Janaway (Cambridge: Cambridge University Press, 2018), § 18.

iv.

Marcel often muses that the preconditions of experience place a restriction on him, as when theorizing that "in all perception there exists a barrier as a result of which there is never absolute contact between reality and our intelligence," for example the "vast fabric of dream" which can bathe the beloved in its warm light.[83] What is here conceived of as a boundary or gap, between the surrounding world and our experience of it, is conceptualized in Pyrrhonian skepticism in terms of "circumstances": that is, "conditions or dispositions."[84] We may be in love or not, grieving or joyful, sober or drunk, but what is impossible is to be in *none* of these conditions, nor in any other(s). This is not to say that we must turn our gaze within and "introspect" to learn what we believe or what emotion we are experiencing: rather, we are more likely to discover this by taking notice of how the world seems (to us) to be.[85] Yet in finding things to be a certain way, we rely upon what Proust's narrator describes as an "environment which itself is invisible but through the translucent and changing medium of which" we see, "that is to say those beliefs," including about issues of value, "which we do not perceive" but which in their invisibility are just as pervasive as is "the air that surrounds us."[86] It is in this sense that all emotional

---

[83] *Time Regained*, III: 1023. As I noted earlier, we should hesitate to take at face value every such theoretical reflection, for example that a variably colored glass stands "between mind and world": see the discussion in Landy, *Philosophy as Fiction*, 51–52. Epistemological despair need not be the last word. Emotional perception, as Nussbaum maintains, "is not like being given a snapshot of the object, but requires looking at the object, so to speak, through one's own window": see *Upheavals of Thought*, 27–28. Again, see the image of a "photographic plate" used in *The Guermantes Way*, II: 142.

[84] Sextus Empiricus, *Outlines of Pyrrhonism*, 1.100.

[85] See Paul Ricoeur, *Freedom and Nature*, trans. Erazim V. Kohák (Evanston, IL: Northwestern University Press, 1966), 10: the "knowledge of subjectivity cannot be reduced to introspection." That an existential philosopher cares about subjectivity, then, does not imply that for him great "epistemic weight [must be] carried by introspection," as Peter Mehl alleges: *Thinking through Kierkegaard* (Urbana, IL: University of Illinois Press, 2005), 59.

[86] *The Captive*, III: 145.

impressions are conditioned by what the skeptic names the subjective "circumstances" of the individual.

How a person is disposed, as phenomenological consensus attests, influences how his or her world is constituted; yet it is still a lens that we look *through*, not *at*. Simply put, "I am not turned toward my affective perspective; on the contrary, it is out of it that things appear interesting to me; and it is upon these things that I grasp the lovable, the attractive, the hateful, the repulsive,"[87] and so on. In other words, "my consciousness is turned primarily toward the world, turned toward things; it is above all a relation to the world."[88] The image of viewing the world through a clear pane of glass has been used to portray a vantage point entirely free of bias,[89] but for reasons we have already seen this ideal is deeply problematic. Besides, even if we always embody a perspective that resembles variably colored glass, are we not still viewing something other than ourselves through it, as opposed to looking at it? Once again, Merleau-Ponty provides insight:

> What has to be understood is, beyond the "persons," the existentials according to which we comprehend them, and which are the sedimented meaning of all our voluntary and involuntary experiences. This unconscious is to be sought not at the bottom of ourselves, behind the back of our "consciousness," but in front of us, as articulations of our field. It is "unconscious" by the fact that it is not an *object* but it is that through which objects are possible.[90]

---

[87] Paul Ricoeur, *Fallible Man*, trans. Charles Kelbley (New York: Fordham University Press, 1986), 51.

[88] Maurice Merleau-Ponty, *The Primacy of Perception*, ed. James M. Edie (Evanston, IL: Northwestern University Press, 1964), 116–117.

[89] See Francis-Noël Thomas and Mark Turner, *Clear and Simple as the Truth* (Princeton, NJ: Princeton University Press, 1994), esp. 55 and 92–93, where they single out Proust as an author for whom the paradigm of a transparent lens is replaced by a "romantic style" that "reveals the self." Cf. George Orwell, "Politics and the English Language," in *A Collection of Essays* (Orlando, FL: Harcourt, Inc., 1946), 156–170.

[90] Merleau-Ponty, *The Visible and the Invisible*, 180.

Our temperamental sensitivity is complex and idiosyncratically formed, so although it provides us with a window onto the world, what is seen is inevitably inflected by our way of seeing. And the most relevant metaphor for this within Proust's novel is the *kaleidoscope*.

Introduced quite early on, as Marcel recalls momentarily waking from sleep and opening his eyes to see the furniture in the dark room through a "shifting kaleidoscope" of drowsiness, this quite evidently indicates an orientation, such as the "silent . . . contentment" with which he watches the water-lilies at one point, or his "melancholy" in contemplating the "boundless field of possibilities" for infidelity that Paris affords to Albertine.[91] A shift in patterns of attention may be characterized as a "turn" of the kaleidoscope, and ideas about politics and religion are often "kaleidoscopic" as well.[92] "As soon as we have a desire to know," our narrator explains, we are employing "a dizzy kaleidoscope in which we can no longer distinguish anything," an eyepiece that continues to shift, as when it is by turns tinted (as it were) "by jealousy and by love" and we interpret things with either suspicion or trust, in the latter case regarding the beloved with such fondness that we even smile affectionately at her bad taste in music.[93] We are always in one mood or another, some subjective "condition" or other, and we never occupy a neutral standpoint from which to evaluate all other standpoints as more or less revelatory.

Let us examine this image. A kaleidoscope includes colored bits of glass that one looks through, not at, and as an optical instrument

---

[91] *Swann's Way*, I: 4 and 185; *The Captive*, III: 87. The very first passage, only a few pages into the narrative, introduces an emphasis on "particular circumstances or modes of vision" which, as Roger Shattuck notes, "never slackens through three thousand pages of text." See *Proust's Binoculars* (Princeton, NJ: Princeton University Press, 1983), 6.

[92] See *Within a Budding Grove*, I: 556-557; *The Guermantes Way*, II: 194; *Time Regained*, III: 929-930. See also Nicolas Grimaldi, *Proust, les horreurs de l'amour* (Paris: PUF, 2008), 88.

[93] *The Fugitive*, III: 529; *The Captive*, III: 303 and 3. Regarding what follows, see Sextus Empiricus, *Outlines of Pyrrhonism*, 1.112-116; Heidegger, *Being and Time*, §§ 29-30 and 68(b). See also Shattuck, *Proust's Binoculars*, 23-24.

it could not work without admitting light from outside. Yet it varies and changes, creating new patterns upon every turn, and the view that it offers is so strongly tinged by its colors that we can observe very little detail of the external world when peering through it, only the fluctuations of light and shade. To use this as an image of affective vision is to conceive of the world that appears to an emotional being as unclear, constantly in flux, hard to discern—perhaps painted, and thereby tainted. An emotional standpoint need not pretend to be a view from nowhere, the philosopher's impossible ideal of observation magically undertaken without a particular observer, "*knowledge without a knowing subject.*"[94] Thus, what it reveals is not an objective world on which the knower lacks any formative effect. We find in Marcel's imagery a worry that, if "what I feel somehow reflects myself, then, so the reasoning goes, [it] can only be biased and partial," and that therefore "emotional consciousness does not mirror reality,"[95] but is akin to the refracting mirrors of an optical instrument that "bejewel" what we see with adornments that are internal to our own minds.

Proust's narrator not only puts forward as a paradigmatic truth about all perception that everyone feels herself to be at the center, regardless of where she is placed,[96] but he also recognizes that the entire history of experiences that have made one into the particular "tissue of contingencies"[97] that one has so far become—with all one's loves, perplexities, and fears—is what lies at the center of each circle. Yet this is what *our* world gets filtered through. Once that has been established, it follows that "the mind organizes experience not

---

[94] Karl Popper, *Objective Knowledge* (Oxford: Clarendon Press, 1972), 109.
[95] Calhoun, "Subjectivity and Emotion," 175–176. See *Swann's Way*, I: 450, on how Gilberte's house is *bejeweled* in Marcel's infra-red sight.
[96] *Within a Budding Grove*, I: 482. See also Merleau-Ponty, *Phenomenology of Perception*, 249: what we perceive "does not partake of pure being," for "as I see it, it is a moment of my individual history," so it "pre-supposes in me sediments left behind from by some previous constitution, so that I am, as a sentient subject, a repository stocked with [wondrous] powers."
[97] I take this phrase from Richard Rorty, *Contingency, Irony, and Solidarity* (Cambridge: Cambridge University Press, 1989), 32.

under a uniform set of transcendentally necessary 'categories' but under a unique perspective dictated by the individual's interests."[98] At one point, after a conversation with Andrée, Marcel observes that, "if differences between minds account for the different impressions produced upon one person and another by the same work, and differences of feeling account for the impossibility of captivating a person who does not love you, there are also differences between characters [and] peculiarities in a single character"—and his conclusion is to remark on "how difficult it is to know the truth in this world."[99] Yet being moved compellingly, for instance by such a piece of music as the one that revives in Swann a belief in higher realities, is throughout the novel a gold standard. Finding it "inconceivable" that "a piece of music which gives us an emotion that we feel to be more exalted [and] more true" does not "correspond to some definite spiritual reality," Proust's protagonist claims that, if it did not, then "life would be meaningless"—reducing to absurdity what he shortly thereafter refers to as "the materialist hypothesis, that of there being nothing," that is, "nothing . . . real" in a beautiful strain of music or the "states of soul" of listeners who are overwhelmingly moved by it.[100] As Marcel ominously states in the latter passage, granted that life's meaning or meaninglessness is what is at stake: "I began to doubt again."

If by chance he had never met Albertine, she would not have been a meaningful person in his life; yet does this imply that in actuality she was "utterly meaningless" to him, or that she "who had been the cause of such an upheaval of my being" counted "for little or nothing" aside from the "chance occurrences" that brought

---

[98] Landy, *Philosophy as Fiction*, 60.
[99] *The Fugitive*, III: 634. Regarding what follows, see *Swann's Way*, I: 230.
[100] *The Captive*, III: 381 and 388. On the sense in which beauty is experienced "as inviting or requiring something from us, a response that may be owed to it," and why this "normativity . . . does not apply either to the pleasure of the agreeable or to ordinary empirical judgments such as those of color," see Moran, *The Philosophical Imagination*, 73–74.

them together?[101] As we saw above, meaning takes shape in relation to chance events, and there is reason to question whether this ought to make us doubt love. Proust's narrator is ambivalent about being, in Nussbaum's terms, "an incomplete creature in a world of significant accidents," and this is related to what he himself admits is an "anxious need to be tyrannical [in] matters of love."[102] Nor is Marcel unaware that his own style of loving may prevent him from recognizing the beloved as she is. If he conceives of his own psyche as a barrier to apprehending reality, it may be due to the "circumstances" highlighted by the ancient skeptics: the fact that we are always in one affective disposition or another, none of which can be taken as authoritative. And if his mind is a dizzy kaleidoscope, it may be due to his tendency to oscillate between distrustful jealousy, which makes him "eager . . . to know" all the "persons, cities, [and] roads" linked with Albertine, and a charitable love that seeks a mitigating, forgiving, explanation of the evidence.[103] When he wonders whether she is being truthful about having walked with a certain person down the street one week ago, he puzzles over what might have been visible if he had been an eye-witness:

> The evidence of my senses, if I had been in the street at that moment, would perhaps have informed me that the lady had not been with Albertine. . . . [Yet] to invoke this evidence by the senses I should have had to be in the street at that particular moment, and I had not been. One can imagine, however, that such a hypothesis is not improbable: I might have gone out, and have been passing along the street at the time at which Albertine was

---

[101] *The Captive*, III: 21; *The Fugitive*, III: 439–440. The "accidental" element that exists even in Marcel's relationship with his grandmother, and in their having spent such memorable times together, is underscored in Samuel Beckett, *Proust* (New York: Grove Press, 1957), 28.

[102] See Nussbaum, *Upheavals of Thought*, 178–181; Proust, *The Captive*, III: 86.

[103] *The Captive*, III: 81–82; again, see *The Captive*, III: 303. That love seeks a "mitigating explanation" is Kierkegaard's claim in *Works of Love*, 290–294. On how we finite beings have, allegedly, "no organ for *knowing*, for 'truth,'" see Nietzsche, *The Gay Science*, § 354.

to tell me in the evening (not having seen me there) that she had walked a few steps with the lady, and I should then have known that Albertine was lying. But is this absolutely certain even then? A strange darkness would have clouded my mind, I should have begun to doubt whether I had seen her alone, I should hardly even have sought to understand by what optical illusion I had failed to perceive the lady, and I should have not been greatly surprised to find myself mistaken, for the stellar universe is not so difficult of comprehension as the real actions of other people, especially of the people we love, fortified as they are against our doubts by fables devised for their protection.[104]

It is little wonder that Proust's narrator finds it difficult to know the truth in this world, compelled as he is to rely upon a fallible optical instrument, an imperfect faculty of apprehension. At the end of a similar inventory of all the subjective factors behind his wish "to know at all costs what Albertine was thinking, whom she saw, whom she loved," he blurts out, exasperated: "Besides, is there any need to know a fact?"[105] Despite the "subjective" nature of his love, Marcel is by virtue of this affective disposition preoccupied with how Albertine spends her time, and with whom. His emotional orientation toward her, idiosyncratic as it may be, makes him want to know actual facts about the surrounding world.

Despite what might appear to be "the purely mental character of reality," Marcel remarks, "the subjective element that I had observed to exist ... in vision itself did not imply that an object could not possess real qualities."[106] It is just that these qualities take on a

---

[104] *The Captive*, III: 187–188. On the curious dialectic of love and jealousy in Proust, see Sartre, *Being and Nothingness*, 235–236.
[105] *The Captive*, III: 92. Regarding what follows, see *The Captive*, III: 14. On "this subjective nature of my love," see *The Fugitive*, III: 568. As for how, despite protestations to the contrary, Marcel endlessly "reminds himself of the independence and reality of the external world," see Jones, *Philosophy and the Novel*, 167–169; see also Bersani, *Marcel Proust: The Fictions of Life and of Art*, 242–243.
[106] *Time Regained*, III: 952–953. Cf. *The Captive*, III: 88.

particular meaning *for him* due to the current state of his singular, contingent perspective. Which inward "circumstances" should he treat as the most reliable? As a skeptic would remind us, it is only from within one disposition or another, such as being jealous or not, that he can even contemplate this question. And once Marcel is cognizant of this, he tends to despair of ever finding the truth. The very same emotional attunement that motivates him to know can also lead him to misconstrue the evidence. Being on alert for any sign of infidelity, he is more likely to pick up on actual indications of this than an impartial, oblivious spectator would. On the other hand, in his fear and worry about losing Albertine he is also liable to view innocuous facts as further incriminating her.

His inquisitorial approach to her, of course, dates back to his first encounter with Albertine, when he is transfixed by her gaze and intrigued by the mystery of the unfamiliar universe hidden behind her eyes. Marcel at the time speaks of longing to *possess* this unknown, enticing world, and of wanting to *unite* his life with hers. We have noted already how his own vision can be distorted by a wish to control the beloved, which is one thing that the language of possession might imply. Yet a gentler connotation would be that he wants to bring her unique mode of being more intimately into his life, which would also explain how their worlds might be unified to some degree—where that means shared, not merged indistinguishably. Rather than projecting onto Albertine a fantasy of his own invention, he wants to know about what specific places she has ridden through on her bicycle, what home she will return to at the end of the day, her plans (formed by herself or by others), along with her desires, her sympathies, her revulsions, and her "obscure and incessant will."[107] Later, while insisting a few times within just two pages that he no longer loved Albertine and had no further interest in

---

[107] *Within a Budding Grove*, I: 851–852. Cf. Nehamas, "Only in the Contemplation of Beauty is Human Life Worth Living," 9–10. See also İlham Dilman, *Love* (New York: St. Martin's Press, Inc., 1998), 60ff.

learning about her, he subverts these claims by carefully recording her alluring habit of responding to something he has said by asking him, "Is that true? Is it really true?"[108] Even through jealous eyes, Marcel delivers a sharp vision of Albertine.

Admittedly, our narrator links even this observation with the possibility that she has greeted "with sensuality" compliments made by other admirers. His possessiveness threatens to prohibit Marcel from loving Albertine in such a way as to make the Murdochian realization "that something other than oneself is real," a "discovery of reality" through love as the apprehension of an independent, separate being.[109] Simone Weil might advise him "to give up being the center of the world in imagination, to discern that all points in the world are equally centers," and this would be fitting advice—yet, in the very process of advocating unselfish neighborly love, Weil also notes that in "the subtle analyses of Proust" we do find a romantic love that is oriented toward the distinct beauty of a person, the texture of her existence.[110] Insofar as Marcel is drawn to this, insofar as he loves Albertine and finds her beautiful, his life will be better with her than without,[111] and he will want to keep discovering more about her. When he speaks of "the terrible deception of love" that it draws us not to an actual "woman of the external world" but with an image of her "fashioned in our brain," by contrast, this is when he is superficially preoccupied with a fantasized version of

---

[108] *The Captive*, III: 13–14. On his "inquisitorial sentiment," which "suffers from knowing," but then "seeks to learn yet more," see *The Captive*, III: 51.

[109] Murdoch, *Existentialists and Mystics*, 215–216. On a person's unique "texture of being" or "their total vision of life," see *Existentialists and Mystics*, 80–81. Cf. Merleau-Ponty, *Phenomenology of Perception*, 381–382, on personal "style," a "certain manner of dealing with situations" which often remains the same "in everything [a person] says and does." See also, for an account of "texture of being," or (in other words) "subjective perspective," Íngrid Vendrell Ferran, *Die Vielfalt der Erkenntis*, 165–170.

[110] Simone Weil, *Waiting for God*, trans. Emma Craufurd (New York: G. P. Putnam's Sons, 1951), 159–160 and (on Proust), 171.

[111] Cf. Nehamas, *Only a Promise of Happiness*, 62–63. He states that "beauty points to the future, and we pursue it without knowing what it will yield," which "makes it as difficult to say why we love someone as it is to say why someone else is our friend."

Mademoiselle Stermaria, whom he doesn't really know.[112] His affective "attitudes" may constitute "a medium the permeability of which is infinitely variable and remains unknown to ourselves," but this does not mean he is "cut off from the 'world,'" that for Marcel the emotional a priori (his subjective circumstances, in Pyrrhonian language) can only manage to conceal the beloved other from oneself.

Proust's fascination with peculiar temperaments, with affective subjectivity, has led to his novel being read as positing that, because "we only really know through our sensibility," therefore "all reality is subjective," where this implies a kind of distortion.[113] One way in which Marcel's perspective *can* be distorting is when, as we were just noting, he replaces the resistance of actual otherness with a pliable, make-believe woman that he has fabricated. We have seen that another kind of distortion in his outlook derives from his attempt to control the beloved for his own purposes. If Albertine can surprise him, as she repeatedly does, this is because her emotional point of view is distinct from his own and therefore beyond his grasp—the narrative recognizes this even when Marcel does not. But even the fact that it is *she* who captivates him, *her* vantage point that he yearns to know, has something to do with Proust's narrator himself. The most selfless attention we can devote to another is nevertheless revelatory of our own subjectivity:[114] this is what Marcel means when he claims that "what we call experience is merely the

---

[112] *The Guermantes Way*, II: 384. Regarding what follows, see *The Guermantes Way*, II: 280–281. On the perceived beauty of the beloved, Sextus Empiricus is (needless to say) skeptical: see *Outlines of Pyrrhonism*, 1.108.

[113] F. C. Green, *The Mind of Proust* (Cambridge: Cambridge University Press, 1949), 398: he presents this as a "familiar Proustian conviction." See also Singer, *The Nature of Love, Volume Three*, 185: for "Proustian lovers," love "is always shown to be a subjective phenomenon that they themselves create but finally destroy because they can no longer believe in its objectivity."

[114] *The Fugitive*, III: 443. On his "type," see *The Fugitive*, III: 512–513; as for his need to control, cf. Nussbaum, *Upheavals of Thought*, 511–519. On how love that eclipses egoistic interests to embrace the truth of another person is a categorically discrete mode of awareness, see Hadreas, *A Phenomenology of Love and Hate*, 35–36. See also Scheler, *The Nature of Sympathy*, 166–170.

revelation to our own eyes of a trait in our character." The exaggeration in this statement can be removed if we replace the word "merely" with "partially."

Later, I will address some of the reasons why one might celebrate the fact that our loves bear witness to our distinctive being, in such a manner that "the universe is real for us all and dissimilar to each of us."[115] For *In Search of Lost Time* contains a powerful evocation of what it is like to affirm perspectival truth, life as we have felt it to be, as well as what philosophical justification there is for doing so. Right now, however, my concern is with the Marcel who favors a positivistic, skeptical, or meaningless interpretation—the one who points out that "we are, when we love, in an abnormal state," in which many accidents that occur seem to have "a seriousness" they themselves would at other times, in other subjective conditions, not possess.[116] The significant accidents, as they once seemed to be, from the latter standpoint have no importance anymore—they are like a word one no longer understands—so, he infers, perhaps things were always empty of meaning, even if it once felt otherwise. And nihilistic skepticism cannot be shown, demonstrably or irrefutably, to rest upon a faulty way of thinking. Speaking about his loss of faith, Proust's narrator writes that "I believed in things and in people while I walked along those paths," at a youthful age, and that this is why "the things and the people they made known to me are the only ones that I still take seriously and that still bring me joy."[117] The "flowers that people show me nowadays for the first time," he sadly admits, no longer "seem to me to be true flowers." This invites us to ask: what was it about his inner "circumstances," at the earlier stage, that made everything seem real? "I believed in things and in

---

[115] *The Captive*, III: 189. Cf. Nietzsche, *Unfashionable Observations*, trans. Richard T. Gray (Stanford, CA: Stanford University Press, 1995), 171ff.

[116] *Within a Budding Grove*, I: 626. See also *The Fugitive*, III: 657–658; *Time Regained*, III: 940–941. On placing "the flag of truth" either in experiences of being engaged with significant matters or in feelings of cosmic absurdity, see Ratcliffe, *Experiences of Depression*, 276–277.

[117] *Swann's Way*, I: 201.

people" back then, he says, alluding to the kind of conviction that has a pervasive influence on how the world appears to be, due to the way it defines what subjective "circumstances" we find ourselves in—that is, how we ourselves are inwardly disposed.

V.

The fifth skeptical mode of suspending judgment is based upon comparing "positions, distances, and locations" from which an observer may regard the world.[118] Approaching the town of Balbec for the first time, Marcel feels himself entering "an unknown and infinitely more interesting universe," which, when glimpsed in person, seems "something less" than he expected based on his romantic anticipations,[119] which themselves were based largely upon Swann's and Legrandin's praise of the place. What seemed so charming from a greater distance appears up close to be lacking in charm—just as the narrator becomes apathetic toward Albertine and her friends (who have preoccupied his attention) when he thinks himself to be on the verge of making their acquaintance for the first time, and he finds that they suddenly seem appealing again when they move away from him and he realizes that he has missed this opportunity. That is a classic illustration of a pattern spelled out by another Proustian narrator in the rhetorical question, "To one who loves, is not absence the most effective, the most tenacious, the most indestructible, the most faithful of presences?"[120] Nearing the end of that summer by the sea, Marcel makes the following observation:

> It is, after all, as good a way as any of solving the problem of existence to get near enough to the things and people that have

---

[118] Sextus Empiricus, *Outlines of Pyrrhonism*, 1.118.
[119] *Within a Budding Grove*, I: 707–710.
[120] "A Young Girl's Confession," in *Pleasures and Regrets*, trans. Louise Varese (Hopewell, NJ: Ecco Press, 1949), 31–47, 32.

appeared to us beautiful and mysterious from a distance to be able to satisfy ourselves that they have neither mystery nor beauty. It is one of the systems of mental hygiene among which we are at liberty to choose our own, [which] gives us a certain tranquillity with which to spend what remains of life, and . . . with which to resign ourselves to death.[121]

As always, there is more to it than his dismissive and cynical remarks would lead us to believe. Nonetheless, Marcel does have a point, as indicated by his allusion to philosophical "systems of mental hygiene" employed to maintain one's peace of mind. Do not give your assent to any apparently meaningful impression, but rather suspend judgment—or perhaps more effective still, convince yourself that it *means* nothing. This has been advocated since ancient times as a way to defend oneself against emotional vulnerability. Although it invites criticism, like any other strategy of defense it is also effective, at least to some degree. The "problem of existence" that it brings us to terms with could be characterized in Proust's own phrase as "the intermittencies of the heart."

As for its truthfulness, on the other hand—this practically efficacious method constitutes a form of dishonesty with oneself. Our narrator at a disenchanted moment reflects that, when a "divine spark" of animating belief within us has gone out, and we no longer can find things wondrous, it feels as if we were experiencing nothing less than "the death of the gods."[122] However, the Marcel who claims that he is finding neither beauty nor mystery in Albertine and her friends is not at all disillusioned. He is in the midst of eight pages in

---

[121] *Within a Budding Grove*, I: 1011, where Marcel refers back to his missed encounter with the young women—see *Within a Budding Grove*, I: 914–919. On protecting oneself against what seems valuable, see also Thomas Baldwin, *The Material Object in the Work of Marcel Proust* (New York: Peter Lang, 2005), 165. On the "intermittencies of the heart," see *Cities of the Plain*, II: 778ff. Finally, regarding the peace of mind sought by Proustian lovers, beginning with Swann, see Derwent May, *Proust* (Oxford: Oxford University Press, 1983), 30–32.

[122] *Swann's Way*, I: 460. Regarding what follows, see also Georges Cattaui, *Marcel Proust*, trans. Ruth Hall (New York: Minerva Press, 1968), 82–83.

which the emotional atmosphere is otherwise enchanted: he sorts, appreciatively, through everything from the personal traits and passions to the shades of color and mood showing in the aspects of Andrée, Gisèle, Rosamonde, and Albertine, leading up to the conclusion that he considers himself as blessed with the divine as if he had been "amid a band of nymphs."[123] The mentally hygienic theory he professes about a lack of mystery and beauty is untrue to his experience. It is something he tells himself, in the attempt to make life seem less burdened with meaning.

The other side of the interplay of closeness and distance that Marcel notices, which corresponds to taking for granted what is near at hand, are the mysterious powers that places or times can harbor, once we are forced to acknowledge the permanent absence *from* them of people we have loved who are there no more. All the mundane features of the room where our protagonist dined with Albertine up to the final evening she was with him take on after her departure a tender beauty that fills his eyes with tears,[124] just as the wall from the other side of which his grandmother had formerly returned his knocks becomes for him unbearably haunted with her loss. Thus does love make space and time "perceptible to the heart," as Marcel comments.[125] He is by no means wandering through an absurd world, like the Bob Dylan who sings, "I've got new eyes / Everything looks far away," in such a manner as to seem distant and indifferent.[126] Proust's narrator is experiencing not the painful gap Camus locates between the human need for meaning and

---

[123] See *Within a Budding Grove*, I: 1005–1013. On affective "atmosphere," see Thomas Fuchs, "The Phenomenology of Affectivity," in *The Oxford Handbook of Philosophy and Psychiatry*, ed. K. W. M. Fulford et al. (New York: Oxford University Press, 2013), 612–628, 616–617.

[124] *The Fugitive*, III: 503–504. On the hotel room wall at Balbec, see *Cities of the Plain*, II: 790.

[125] *The Captive*, III: 391–392.

[126] Bob Dylan, "Highlands," in *Lyrics, 1962–2001* (New York: Simon & Schuster, 2004), 571–573. A less absurd, more tragic sense returns, e.g., in "Sugar Baby," one album later and on page 597 of the same volume: "Every moment of existence seems like some dirty trick / Happiness can come suddenly and leave just as quick."

"the silence of the world," nor the "divorce between the mind that desires and the world that disappoints."[127] Marcel's environment is rich with significance, and the "mental hygiene" he seeks to practice aims to deprive the world of its value, which he has plainly felt.

In other words, Marcel emphatically inhabits what Husserl after his existential turn describes as the "surrounding world," one that is replete with human meaning—*not* a mathematically abstracted realm of objects from which the "relativity of subjective interpretations" has been artificially stripped.[128] Instead, the power of subjectivity is extended to include the entire totality of the world.[129] Conscious of Albertine's existence "only when I set eyes on her," he nevertheless does not sincerely regard her as an indifferent object, located in an axiologically neutral space.[130] She is a *subject*, and could not torment him as she often does if she had no mind of her own, no inner depths—which, when partially glimpsed, are "so precious a revelation of her life that, for the privilege of exploring that underlying world, we would gladly sacrifice our own."[131] Another time, when he watches her sleep, it occurs to Marcel that her body, "stretched out to the infinity of all the points that it had occupied in space and time," was "capable of causing

---

[127] Albert Camus, *The Myth of Sisyphus and Other Essays*, trans. Justin O'Brien (New York: Vintage Books, 1991), 28–30 and 49–50. That this ought to be felt as a "terrifying" plight is convincingly argued by Karen L. Carr in *The Banalization of Nihilism* (Albany, NY: SUNY Press, 1992), 119–121.

[128] Edmund Husserl, *The Crisis of European Sciences and Transcendental Phenomenology*, trans. David Carr (Evanston, IL: Northwestern University Press, 1970), 23–29 and 272–295 (the latter is from his "Vienna Lecture"). Cf. Heidegger, *Being and Time*, §§ 14–19 and 44. See also Stephen Mulhall, *Inheritance and Originality* (Oxford: Clarendon Press, 2001), 235–238.

[129] Cf. Anne Henry, *Proust* (Paris: Éditions Balland, 1986), 210.

[130] *The Captive*, III: 130. I disagree with Gabriel Marcel, who claims that, "for Proust, the thou is instantly converted into an it." See *Creative Fidelity*, trans. Robert Rosthal (New York: Farrar, Straus and Company, 1964), 72. Cf. Langton, "Love and Solipsism," 143–144: "In treating Albertine as something to be possessed, . . . Marcel treats her as a thing."

[131] *The Captive*, III: 109–110.

me . . . so intense an anguish."[132] Meditating along similar lines about locations and distances, he elsewhere says:

> I realized the impossibility which love comes up against. We imagine that it has as its object a being that can be laid down in front of us, enclosed within a body. Alas, it is the extension of that being to all the points in space and time that it has occupied and will occupy. If we do not possess its contact with this or that place, this or that hour, we do not possess that being. But we cannot touch all these points.[133]

Another person appears in a certain "position, relative to ourselves," not only in the sense of being (e.g., to our left), but based upon our acquaintance with her, be it intimate or casual or nonexistent. And compared with the latter type of difference in position, Proust's hero asserts, "there is perhaps nothing [else] that gives us so strong an impression of the reality of the external world."[134] The body of his beloved can seem, "from a few yards, from a few inches away, remote from us." Yet if a "violent change" is brought about in its position in relation to us, for instance if we are shown "that it is in love with others and not with us," then "by the beating of our shattered heart we feel that" it is "within us that the beloved creature was."[135] And it is a painful change of location that takes place when someone lodged in our heart suddenly becomes more distant.

---

[132] See *The Captive*, III: 366–367; see also *The Captive*, III: 95, a scene in which he is calling Andrée to seek information about Albertine. The joy of coming to know something about the beloved persists despite how disturbing the truth is that he learns.
[133] *The Captive*, III: 95; see also *The Fugitive*, III: 609–615.
[134] *Within a Budding Grove*, I: 716. On love as an "epistemic practice," which can "take us closer to rather than further from the truth," as it requires charitable attention, not that "one completely divorce oneself from reality," see Jollimore, *Love's Vision*, 64–70. Cf. Margaret Olivia Little, "Seeing and Caring: The Role of Affect in Feminist Moral Epistemology," 118–124.
[135] *Cities of the Plain*, II: 1165. See *Cities of the Plain*, II: 1153–1154.

"Such people, while they change in relation to ourselves, change also in themselves." The beloved other "does not stay still"; rather, she moves and shifts.[136] Prior to making the acquaintance of Albertine, Marcel found that she "seemed to exist on a parallel plane to that on which I was living," like a "great actress" on the "blazing beach" in front of the hotel at Balbec. Yet before long their planes converge, and when she ends up living at his Paris residence she is a wild bird that has been captured, to whose company he has become accustomed to such an extent that he feels "that vague impression of her that we have of our own limbs," as if she were right beside him, even when in fact she is not: no wonder, then, that Proust's narrator finds himself persistently failing to see her adequately.[137] Albertine herself never ceases to undergo variations, like any other temporal being. In her process of becoming, she provides an inconstant target to the Marcel who longs to know her.

"Each time, a [woman] so little resembles what she was the time before," he laments, "that the stability of nature which we ascribe to her is purely fictitious." In the same paragraph, Marcel rhapsodizes:

> In themselves, what were Albertine and Andrée? To know the answer, I should have to immobilize you, to cease to live in that perpetual state of expectancy ending always in a different presentment of you, I should have to cease to love you in order to fix your image.[138]

---

[136] I cite *The Captive*, III: 63; then, *Within a Budding Grove*, I: 528. What follows is from *The Captive*, III: 61–62. Cf. J. E. Rivers, *Proust and the Art of Love* (New York: Columbia University Press, 1980), 103, on Proust's "realization that the self is a perpetually changing entity."

[137] *The Captive*, III: 334. She is, at the moment he makes this remark, not actually present, but awaiting him back home as he has been out at a party. Cf. René Descartes, *Meditations on First Philosophy*, 3rd edition, trans. Donald A. Cress (Indianapolis: Hackett Publishing Company, 1993), 50: "I had sometimes heard it said by people whose leg or arm had been amputated that it seemed to them that they still occasionally sensed pain in the very limb they had lost" (Sixth Meditation). On Marcel's repeated failures to apprehend some aspects of reality, see Deleuze, *Proust and Signs*, 181.

[138] *The Captive*, III: 58–59. On characterological fluctuation, see John Doris, *Lack of Character* (Cambridge: Cambridge University Press, 2002), 15–20.

The beloved other exists in a state of Heraclitean flux that presents many sides to us over time; and, bearing witness to all that has moved us about her in the past, she embodies a palimpsest of meanings—some of them, from distant history, capable of becoming salient any moment. Meanwhile, we ourselves undergo alterations that can be imperceptible to us. "The heart changes, and it is our worst sorrow," as Marcel remarks, but "its alteration, like that of certain natural phenomena, is so gradual that, even if we are able to distinguish, successively, each of its different states, we are still spared the actual sensation of change."[139] We know that, years ago, we were indifferent to the same person who now holds our heart in her hands. Marcel bemusedly recalls how he once missed an opportunity to meet Albertine much earlier, the evening when he decided against joining his father for a dinner which, in the company of her aunt, Madame Bontemps, Albertine was attending.

"So it is that the different periods of our life overlap one another. We scornfully decline, because of one whom we love," namely Gilberte at this stage, "to see another," that is, Albertine, "whom we might perhaps, had we consented to see her now, have loved a little sooner and who would thus have put a term to our present sufferings, bringing others, it is true, in their place"—the last part of which he adds with a characteristically tragic sensibility.[140]

Contrary to what he repeatedly insists, for instance that "we simply project" onto the beloved "a state of our own soul," such that what matters is *not* the "worth" of the person we love; or analogously, that "love places in a person who is loved what exists only in the person who loves,"[141] our narrator keeps having encounters

---

[139] *Swann's Way*, I: 92.
[140] *Within a Budding Grove*, I: 674. On "the thousands of [affective] threads" that "keep us bound to the world," see Arthur Schopenhauer, *The World as Will and Representation, Volume One*, trans. Judith Norman, Alistair Welchman, and Christopher Janaway (Cambridge: Cambridge University Press, 2010), § 68.
[141] I cite *Within a Budding Grove*, I: 891–892; then, *Time Regained*, III: 950–951. Time and time again for Proust's narrator, as Merleau-Ponty points out, "life gives us something other than what we were searching for." *Institution and Passivity*, 44. Cf. May, *Proust*, 26: "The realization of the independent existence of the outside world always has some

with a world whose features and contours are elusive and surprising. Albertine is not colorless but multicolored, her tints always shifting like those of a dove's or pigeon's neck—to rely on an example used by Sextus Empiricus, of how things appear different from one angle than they do from another.[142] But we are so often pained by the varied alterations of those whom we love, as we are not by the colorful necks of doves—and through this painful suffering, we encounter reality. When the lover Marcel tries to apprehend the beloved Albertine, invariably he can do so only as Marcel *at time X*, perceiving Albertine *at time X*, and *from angle Y*, with his particular attunement and concerns toward her *at* that time and *from* that angle.[143] He seems to heed Nietzsche's warning against "the ridiculous immodesty of decreeing from our angle that perspectives are *permitted* only from this angle." As individuals we are each a succession of variants of ourselves, always revealing a new face as we undergo another transformation, each one "giving birth to new perspectives" from which the world gets articulated in one or another configuration.[144] As any Pyrrhonian skeptic could tell Marcel (or any Stoic, for that matter), affective attachments to changeable

---

such effect on Marcel. It alarms and upsets him, as his earlier fantasy loses control." See also Kubala, "Love and Transience in Proust," 544: Marcel's "solipsistic" maxims are refuted by his other "thoughts and actions." This rightly opposes the common view that the Proustian beloved is *merely* our subjective creation: see, e.g., Louis Gautier-Vignal, *Proust, connu et inconnu* (Paris: Éditions Robert Laffont, 1976), 235. Rather, it is possible for us "to know what another person sees" of a universe unlike our own. *Time Regained*, III: 932.

[142] Sextus Empiricus, *Outlines of Pyrrhonism*, 1.120. In connection with what follows, see Julia Kristeva, *Time and Sense: Proust and the Experience of Literature*, trans. Ross Guberman (New York: Columbia University Press, 1996), 252–255; Rosset, *Joyful Cruelty: Toward a Philosophy of the Real*, 77: "suffering knows more about reality" than other modes of apprehension.
[143] Cf. Landy, *Philosophy as Fiction*, 121–122. The following sentence is from Nietzsche, *The Gay Science*, § 374.
[144] Rawlinson, "Art and Truth: Reading Proust," 10. On the "articulation" of the world see Merleau-Ponty, *Phenomenology of Perception*, 35, 203, 292, 301, and 346. Shattuck writes of Proust's notion of "personality as intermittent," saying: "We cannot be all of ourselves all at once." *Proust's Binoculars*, 67–68. That the self is a *series* of selves is mentioned also by Beckett: *Proust*, 8; see also Rivers, *Proust and the Art of Love*, 195. The ensuing passage is from Sextus Empiricus, *Outlines of Pyrrhonism*, 3.236–238.

beings dispose us to become "disquieted in various ways." That is to say, "love toward a thing subject to considerable instability, a thing which we can never possess," entails "emotional distress"—because "nobody is disturbed or anxious about any thing unless he loves it."[145] Marcel's love for Albertine, like Charles Swann's for Odette, clearly follows this pattern—regardless of which system of mental hygiene Proust's narrator wishes to adopt.

The laws about how the mind works (Marcel's mind, that is) regarding distances and positions have now been specified, at least in their prevailing tendencies. The beloved when distant or absent seems "sweeter and more beautiful," and much less interesting when close at hand:[146] so Albertine appears intriguing and boring by turns. In a sad, chronic dishonesty of the heart, we value what we lack at the expense of what we have. As Merleau-Ponty writes, commenting on Proust, "one loves nothing but the absent."[147] And, because absence is so exalted, the logic of the narrator's imagery compels him to believe that her beauty as glimpsed from afar is akin to "a mirage," exemplifying the specific kind of "exquisite mirage which love projects."[148] How is it possible to reconcile a remark of this sort with all the evidence in favor of the claim made by Deleuze

---

[145] Spinoza, *Ethics*, 211–212 (Part V, "Scholium" to Proposition 22). One rule of Proust's universe is that "we do not tremble except for ourselves, or for those whom we love." *Swann's Way*, I: 348.

[146] *The Fugitive*, III: 470; then, by way of contrast, *The Captive*, III: 130. Landy reminds us again that "we would be ill advised ... to imagine that all of the sweeping statements we read about love are supposed to apply to everyone" as opposed to only to the narrator, and those who resemble him in the relevant respect. "The Texture of Proust's Novel," in *The Cambridge Companion to Proust*, ed. Richard Bales (Cambridge: Cambridge University Press, 2001), 117–134, 126. See also Landy, *Philosophy as Fiction*, 32–33: one defining particularity of Marcel is to keep hunting for universal laws. Cf. Joshua Landy, "Why a Novel?," in *Proust's "In Search of Lost Time,"* ed. Katherine Elkins (New York: Oxford University Press, 2023), 19–46.

[147] Merleau-Ponty, *Institution and Passivity*, 37.

[148] *The Fugitive*, III: 696. Cf. Grimaldi, *Proust, les horreurs de l'amour*, 180. It is due to statements of this sort that some Proust critics argue that his narrator "could not provide a bleaker analysis of the nature of love: it is an illusion." Richard Bales, *Proust* (London: Grant and Cutler Ltd., 1995), 63. On the distance that opens up "between subject and object," in other words, "narrator and world," see Thomas Baldwin, *Roland Barthes: The Proust Variations* (Liverpool: Liverpool University Press, 2019), 33.

among other Proust interpreters, that À la recherche is above all "a search for truth"?[149] What about the Marcel who reports, after an experience of overwhelming emotion about having lost his grandmother and her infinite and unconditional love forever, that "if I ever did extract some truth from life, it could only be from such an impression"?[150]

Evidently, one motive of Proust's hero is to protect himself from being vulnerable. To put it plainly, "people we love invariably cause us pain,"[151] and this is why Marcel regards it as unfortunate that "we carry inside us that little organ which we call the heart, . . . which we ought to be able to have surgically removed." In light of this, it is in his interest to argue for "the purely subjective nature of the phenomenon that we call love," in which the lover can "superimpose" on the beloved whatever meaning he or she wishes,[152] including no meaning at all. For the sake of gaining emotional control, he continues being drawn as if magnetically back to "the materialist hypothesis, that of there being nothing."[153] Acting in accordance with this would qualify, not as suspending judgment, but as embracing a "dogmatic" skepticism, construing value or significance as a false human imposition.[154] And agnosticism (about the meanings by which we are emotionally moved) is not to be conflated with nihilism.

---

[149] Deleuze, *Proust and Signs*, 94.
[150] *Cities of the Plain*, II: 787.
[151] Kristeva, *Time and Sense*, 254. The following passage is from *The Captive*, III: 224. See also Joel M. Childers, "Proust, Sartre, and the Idea of Love," *Philosophy and Literature* 37 (2013): 389–404, 393–394.
[152] *Within a Budding Grove*, I: 505 and 917–918.
[153] The "materialist hypothesis" is formulated, for instance, in *The Captive*, III: 388. Apparently opposed to it, but also (in Marcel's hands) tending to undermine the world's reality, is "subjective idealism, pure phenomenalism." *Within a Budding Grove*, I: 874.
[154] In *Outlines of Pyrrhonism* 1.1–4, Sextus Empiricus is careful to distinguish the two, and to disassociate himself from the "dogmatic" skeptics. On how to apply this elusive distinction see, e.g., Michael Frede, *Essays in Ancient Philosophy* (Minneapolis: University of Minnesota Press, 1987), 201–222. The nihilistic implications of skepticism about meaning are pointed out by David E. Cooper in *Meaning* (Montreal: McGill-Queen's University Press, 2003), 64.

When our narrator claims of Albertine that "she is my creation," what he means is not that he has invented her out of nothing but that in certain ways, such as her manner of speaking for instance, she "has been profoundly influenced by me."[155] We will recall how Swann wanted to share in Odette's tastes, her habits, and her ideas—an example of how someone who loves wishes to keep discovering, and being influenced by, the beloved. About this very example, Alexander Nehamas claims:

> Not only in love but also in friendship, my desire to possess you is sometimes inseparable from the desire to be possessed by you. At such moments, I don't approach you with a settled sense of myself, taking my plans and my wishes for granted and counting on your assistance with them. Instead, I expect them—I want them—to change once I expose them to you. I hope that you will make me wish for what I have never wished before and give me what I now can't even imagine. You are no longer merely a means to my own ends, which are already established without reference to you, but someone whose own ends can become mine—an end in yourself. I then act on a sense—vague but intense—that there is more to you than I can now see and that it would be better for me to learn what I suspect you can offer. I willingly give you power over myself emotionally.[156]

Because it is precisely this bestowal of emotional power that Marcel tries to resist, it may be telling that he portrays Albertine as *his* creation, and not he hers, so that we are invited to conclude that it is A who loves M,[157] not necessarily the other way around. Yet,

---

[155] *The Captive*, III: 125.
[156] Nehamas, *Only a Promise of Happiness*, 56–57.
[157] "My darling Marcel" (or "my darling _____") is how Albertine tends to greet him upon awakening: see, e.g., *The Captive*, III: 69 and 110. Once again, see Landy, *Philosophy as Fiction*, 22–23. As de Beistegui points out, "reality always seems to have the last word" in spite of Marcel's theories. See *Proust as Philosopher*, 12. Also, it is not only this "A" who loves and has for that reason been influenced by "M": Andrée is also noted to have been influenced by certain traits of his. *The Captive*, III: 12.

although no reader of Proust could honestly state that Albertine's "darling M" is concerned to possess her *only* in this manner, he *is* forced even despite himself to acknowledge her otherness, her subjectivity, which he relentlessly yearns to know—*while also* knowing that he *could* be wrong about what she thinks and feels. This is not within his power to invent or control. Was she happy living with him, or longing for her freedom? "Which of these two hypotheses was the truth?," he asks himself, adding: "I tried to understand Albertine's true state of mind."[158] If she is evasive, it might be because she "had divined the existence in me of an inquisitorial sentiment that desires to know, suffers from knowing, and seeks to learn yet more."[159] If she were only his creation, a blank page on which he could impose whatever he desires, then *La prisonnière* in particular would be a much shorter, and far less interesting, volume than it is. The narrator does have a point when he begrudgingly concedes, "where I had been wrong was perhaps in not making a greater effort to know Albertine in herself."[160] Yet we must be careful not to assume that what Marcel means in saying this is that love is *simply* a matter of accurately tracking lovable qualities, about which one can be objectively "correct."

For a lover and a beloved do, and should, transform themselves through their engagement with one another. Albertine and Marcel are hardly self-contained, prefabricated entities: rather, they develop and change as their love affair acquires a history. The relationship is "an exact, nonrepeatable thing," which has its own significance, "enriched by years of intimacy, of conversation, of letters written and received," and "the love is in large measure

---

[158] *The Captive*, III: 367.
[159] *The Captive*, III: 51.
[160] *The Fugitive*, III: 505–506. As for the objective "correctness" of love, one prominent advocate is Franz Brentano. See *The Origin of Our Knowledge of Right and Wrong*, trans. Roderick M. Chisholm and Elizabeth H. Schneewind (New York: Humanities Press, 1969), 144–147. Marcel's evident use of Kantian *Ding an sich* language hints that he is at this instant trying to factor his own subjective vantage point out of the equation, so to speak.

constituted out of this history."[161] The world of others, in particular of especially beloved others, is a prime illustration of how what surrounds us is neither a fixed, ready-made world nor a meaningless one. Proust's novel bears witness to the axiological facets of reality that his narrator often denies. Indeed, it is an "extraordinarily keen anatomy of a world of meanings," those of gestures, conversations, flowers, annoyances, train rides, cities and seacoasts, characters' quirks, obsessions, absences, and so forth—in sum, a world that, "though a literary creation, is one from whose exploration we easily return, our sensitivity to meanings enhanced, to our own world."[162] The Proustian literary task of narrating all of the above in exceptionally intricate, nuanced detail is a performance of what existential phenomenologists refer to as describing the world "in such a way that its meanings emerge," thus "bringing truth into being" and achieving "a disclosure of the world."[163] What we apprehend is elicited by our emotionally involved, imaginative participation. In Scheler's words, the world is given to us in lived experience as the "bearer of values" because we approach it with the "phenomenological attitude," which lets us "see or experience something which otherwise remains hidden."[164] I noted in my preface that Proust

---

[161] Nussbaum, *Love's Knowledge*, 320–321. I apply to Proust's narrative what she formulates in a different context, but its pertinence here is obvious.

[162] Cooper, *Meaning*, 107–108. Cf. Proust, *The Captive*, III: 381, on how certain emotions (aesthetic ones, for instance) must "correspond to some definite spiritual reality, or life would be meaningless." Also, although Cooper does not mention the following passage either, he would seem to be alluding to a famous Proustian metaphor: "In reality every reader is, while he is reading, the reader of his own self. The writer's work is merely a kind of optical instrument which he offers to the reader to enable him to discern what, without this book, he would perhaps never have perceived." *Time Regained*, III: 949.

[163] I cite, first, Mary Warnock, *Existentialism* (Oxford: Oxford University Press, 1970), 136; then, Merleau-Ponty, *Phenomenology of Perception*, xxii–xxiii. "Because we are in the world," he adds, "we are *condemned to meaning*." Warnock is describing what the "existential philosopher" attempts to do, while Merleau-Ponty is defining what "phenomenology" *is*. Regarding what follows, see also Mooney, *Knights of Faith and Resignation*, 93: "meaning *dawns*, comes to us unbidden," yet it sometimes "appears so *apt* to our particular subjective needs and aspirations" that it almost seems to "have been chosen" by us.

[164] Scheler, "Phenomenology and the Theory of Cognition," in his *Selected Philosophical Essays*, 136–201, 137–143. The notion that Proust is himself a

has frequently been designated a kind of phenomenologist—and there are good reasons for this, one of which is that his poetic prose enacts and captures a value-saturated world.

Except, that is, when it is expressing doubts as to whether life is meaningful; when, in Beckett's terms, Proust's "impressionism" is replaced by his "positivism,"[165] and his narrator adopts the standpoint of a scientist of life, asserting, for example, "the truth of the axiom that matter is indifferent and that anything can be grafted upon it by thought."[166] When Marcel says this, he is thinking specifically about how someone like Rachel appears different close at hand than from a greater distance, and (more importantly) different if one is in love with her than if one is not. In trying to persuade him to abandon his meaning-skepticism, we could point out that it is phenomenologically implausible to say that there exists a bare, neutral world upon which we overlay meanings that are real only in our minds. We could claim, as I did earlier, that what surrounds us is a realm of significance which the "materialist hypothesis" artificially negates.[167] And that, as a literary artist, he or his creator is charged with *vindicating* the worth of human existence, defending how things appear to us when we are emotionally attuned as loving,

---

phenomenologist is, as noted earlier, advocated by Kundera in *The Art of the Novel*, 32; see also, e.g., Baldwin, *The Material Object in the Work of Marcel Proust*, 55.

[165] Beckett, *Proust*, 65.

[166] Proust, *Time Regained*, III: 948. "The *perspectival* law of feeling" which dictates that "what is closest" differs in size and weight from what is "in the distance" is defined by Nietzsche in *The Gay Science*, § 162. On Rachel's appearance up close and farther away, see *The Guermantes Way*, II: 177–178.

[167] Cf. Husserl, *Ideas Pertaining to a Pure Phenomenology and to a Phenomenological Philosophy, Second Book*, 192 and 250. More plausible than talking of "value positings," according to Heidegger too, is acknowledging that "with respect to that which matters most to us (the paradigm case being love), what we care about most is not entirely up to us, not simply within our power to control," which is arguably "a crucial part of what makes it so important." Iain D. Thomson, *Heidegger, Art, and Postmodernity* (Cambridge: Cambridge University Press, 2011), 104. Proust himself occasionally seems to agree: see, e.g., *Selected Letters, 1880–1903*, ed. Philip Kolb, trans. Ralph Manheim (Garden City, NY: Doubleday & Co., 1983), 85: "One loves people because one can't help it."

caring subjects.[168] Indeed, the narrator himself realizes this, for example when he observes:

> I can think of nothing that can to so great a degree as a kiss evoke out of what we believed to be a thing with one definite aspect, the hundred other things which it may equally well be, since each is related to a no less legitimate perspective.[169]

As he leans nearer and nearer to kiss Albertine, he "draws out" more and more of "all the possibilities that [she] contains." What we are faced with here is a fecund proliferation of meanings, a Nietzschean "new infinite" consisting of multifarious available interpretations,[170] each corresponding to a legitimate perspective. As we shall explore further in later chapters, any stance we occupy provides us with a selective, and thus inescapably *partial*, awareness. More often than not, Marcel tends to consider it a pity that things show us "only a limited number of their innumerable attributes, because of the paucity of our senses. They are colored because we have eyes; how many other epithets would they not merit if we had hundreds of senses?"[171] Yet we cannot look through every

---

[168] Why this should be the aim of a "philosophizing poet," and of a literary work of art, is delineated by James D. Reid in *Being Here is Glorious: On Rilke, Poetry, and Philosophy* (Evanston, IL: Northwestern University Press, 2015), 33–34. Cf. Ruth Rebecca Tietjen, "Mystical Feelings and the Process of Self-Transformation," *Philosophia* 45 (2017): 1623–1634, 1624. Speaking also of Rilke, she notes the "phenomenal and evaluative qualities" which are lost on us "if we take a purely scientific stance on the world," such that the poet "encourages us to take a different perspective." On being attuned to existence as meaningful, see also Tietjen, *Am Abgrund: Philosophische Theorie der Angst und Übung in philosophischer Freiheit* (Paderborn: mentis, 2019), 246–249; she cites Heidegger, *Being and Time*, §§ 29–30, 40, and 68.

[169] *The Guermantes Way*, II: 378–379. On how love "is partial" in any event, see *The Captive*, III: 127.

[170] Nietzsche, *The Gay Science*, § 374. With reference to another existential philosopher, José Ferrater Mora explains: "Perspectivistic truth, although partial," is "the only way of seizing reality" for a finite being. It "fails only to be complete." *Ortega y Gasset: An Outline of His Philosophy* (London: Bowes & Bowes, 1956), 30–32.

[171] *The Fugitive*, III: 699. "Perspectives are both *limiting* and *contingent*, and thus afford their inhabitants an essentially *partial* grasp of the world." Plus, "a perspective *favors* some things over others," by virtue of which it is "the opposite of *impartial*." See

window, nor every *kind* of window, at once—and if we sought to do so, we would cancel out the views afforded us from a (that is, from *each*) specific affective standpoint. A *partial* perspective shows us the world *in part*, as viewed in a *partial*, as in *emotionally biased*, way.

That someone "with no imagination" would fail to appreciate the beauty of a specific person, as Proust's narrator remarkably admits,[172] could indicate simply that the subjective faculty of imagination is a condition of possibility for apprehending beauty. We may rely on it even when we find ourselves *involuntarily* spellbound with someone's or something's beauty. Like any other axiological quality, any variety of meaning or significance, beauty is essentially contestable. Facing the naked sea on his first morning at the Grand Hotel, anticipating a walk along the Balbec shore later that day, Marcel takes in the ocean, "bounded by a thin, fluctuating line" formed by "the waves that leapt up one behind another like jumpers on a trampoline," undulating "in a transparent, vaporous, bluish distance."[173] He is emotionally affected, but does what he perceives require a Sartrean "magical transformation of the world"? Maybe so—after all, we cannot decisively silence a skeptic who continues to insist that someone who does not like "the fact that the hotel faces the sea" could "without contradiction say that the hotel faced the sea but was not for that reason a good one."[174] Or, in other words, that appearances of beauty may be capricious or temperamental. But then the overwhelming question becomes: what sort of magic might it be worth our while to believe in?

R. Lanier Anderson, "The Psychology of Perspectivism," *Journal of Nietzsche Studies* 49 (2018): 221–228, 222.

[172] See *The Fugitive*, III: 447. See also Immanuel Kant, *Critique of Judgment*, trans. Werner S. Pluhar (Indianapolis: Hackett Publishing Company, 1987), §§ 17, 49, and 53. Cf. Falck, *Myth, Truth, and Literature*, 34–37.
[173] *Within a Budding Grove*, I: 723. On emotions as magical transformations of the world, see Jean-Paul Sartre, *The Emotions: Outline of a Theory*, trans. Bernard Frechtman (New York: Citadel Press, 1993), 58–83.
[174] R. M. Hare, *Sorting Out Ethics* (Oxford: Clarendon Press, 1997), 70. He is not, I gather, thinking of Proust.

vi.

That we tend to experience things in "admixtures" is named by the Pyrrhonian skeptic as the next mode of suspending judgment. We always perceive things along with other things, none of them impinging upon our senses alone by itself, or so the claim goes.[175] This immediately calls to mind our narrator's longings, the first summer at Balbec, for one after another of Albertine's friends, as he yearns for all of them and not for any of them in particular. Letting his attention alight on each one, he appreciates their beauty complementarily, one of their words or gestures appearing more intriguing as another withdraws, but he does not yet form a clear picture of them.[176] The atmosphere of the seaside resort also influences Marcel's perception of the young women, so that even once Albertine is "cloistered away" in his house far from Balbec, she is still associated with the magic of the coast:[177] "behind this girl, as behind the purple light that used to filter beneath the curtains of my room at Balbec, while outside the concert blared, there shone the blue-green undulations of the sea." How much of her charm was Albertine's own, how much was it "Albertine-at-Balbec," or "having been taken away from Balbec"? The narrator cannot know, although he hints that *some* of her intrigue seems to drain away insofar as she is removed from the beach. Nor is that all. Slices of time are part of what he sees, in seeing her against the seacoast or away from it. The Albertine who had never kissed him would become Albertine his beloved, the girl at Balbec would become the one who had decided to leave him and return to the home of her aunt, soon to be followed by the one who was gone forever. In the midst of

---

[175] Sextus Empiricus, *Outlines of Pyrrhonism*, 1.124–128.
[176] *Within a Budding Grove*, I: 1005–1007.
[177] *The Captive*, III: 61–62. Cf. Irving Singer, *The Nature of Love, Volume Three* (Chicago: University of Chicago Press, 1987), 182–183 and 198, on the significance of Marcel glimpsing Albertine "in this particular landscape," near a window "that discloses the ocean."

one of his earliest soliloquies in honor of an Albertine he so far has barely met, defining what he looks back on as a timeless instant, Marcel turns as it were with a lump in his throat to foreshadow her demise: "When walking with the others she would often stop, forcing her friends, who seemed greatly to respect her, to stop also. Thus it is, coming to a halt, her eyes sparkling," that "I see her again to-day, silhouetted against the screen which the sea spreads out behind her," and separated from him "by a transparent sky-blue space, the interval of time that has elapsed since then."[178] Newly dawning love is haunted by the knowledge of loss, as if doomed already from the start in Proust's universe.

But why should we not recall an earlier impression of a person fated to die young in *light* of their death, once it has taken place? One is perceiving more, not less, of the truth in this case—as when we continue to discern in an adult's face their youthful features, or register a thought of "how little I knew" at a first brief encounter what a truly beloved friend this person would become, and I both view them now *and* remember our earlier meeting in light of a larger meaning that has come to be.[179] The power of a hotel wall on which one's now deceased grandmother had tapped from the other side *affords* one first an environmental solicitation to communicate that way, and later a ghostly aura of past tappings. The wall between the two rooms is not only its material composition but filled with an emotional history, as the past year's experiences there also inhabit it now. In the spirit of this quality, *admixture*, a living relationship is mixed with a bereavement. The very same wall provokes Marcel to feel unable to bear the thought of reaching out a hand in

---

[178] *Within a Budding Grove*, I: 888. Intervals of time are envisioned here as blue in color, like the sky and the sea.

[179] Referring to *The Fugitive*, III: 541, Troy Jollimore observes that, often, "the superimposition of memories and imaginings makes a perceptual experience more complete, more accurate, more profound," and thus does not necessarily invent or obfuscate details. "Love and the Past (and Present, and Future)," in *Philosophy of Love in the Past, Present, and Future*, ed. André Grahle, Natasha McKeever, and Joe Saunders (New York: Routledge, 2022), 94–95.

that direction any more than he could endure to put his hand on "a piano on which my grandmother had been playing and which still vibrated with her touch."[180] Her affectionate greeting inhabits the wall, remarkable in its absence, just as the presence of last summer is there in the room, while *not there* simultaneously.

As with the sense, upon waking up in a room with bodily memories of waking up in other rooms, that to find one's bearings is not easy, likewise a newcomer to the Grand Hotel unaware of the story behind the affordances would be unconscious of what significance that wall holds for Proust's protagonist—simply unable to discern it. Yet it is a feature of this room to bear a sedimented history, in the form of the value qualities that make a claim upon the narrator and prompt him to respond. It is the *unfamiliar* Grand Hotel room that once led Marcel to comment that "it is our noticing them that puts things in a room, our growing used to them that takes them away again and clears a space for us." At first, the room in Balbec was "full of things which did not know me, which flung back at me the distrustful glance I showed at them."[181] It turns into the room where he experiences the kindness of his grandmother and later suffers the disruption of learning what it means to have lost her. The previous summer of being here is not *all* that is here *this* summer, but it is an important part of what is here now. This is why the room affords certain possibilities, not others, and solicits the responses that it evokes in terms of the narrator's present existence.[182] This particular environment offers meaningfully valenced

---

[180] *Cities of the Plain*, II: 790. On what follows, namely how memory informs the way a place feels, see de Beistegui, *Proust as Philosopher*, 30–32; see also, e.g., *Swann's Way*, I: 6–7.

[181] *Within a Budding Grove*, I: 717–719. That it was this room "in which I had experienced my grandmother's kindness, then realized that she was dead," is acknowledged in *Cities of the Plain*, II: 1163–1164.

[182] On affordances, see James J. Gibson, *The Ecological Approach to Visual Perception* (Hillsdale, NJ: Lawrence Erlbaum Associates, 1986), esp. 127–129. See also Joel Krueger and Giovanna Colombetti, "Affective Affordances and Psychopathology," *Discipline Philosophiche* 28, no. 2 (2018): 221–247. About the modes in which "the world, being-in-the-world—Rilke calls it life—leaps toward us from the things," including all that is *actually* in a wall based upon our "comportmental relationship to it," see Martin Heidegger,

opportunities to him: and each "affordance" is "neither an objective property nor a subjective property," but something there to be met with, defined in terms of a relationship of implication between world and self. In this manner life, or being-in-the-world, proffers its qualities toward us.

And these qualities are liable to conflict. As his grandmother's remembered gentleness seems like evidence that contradicts her present nonexistence, in recalling Albertine the narrator remarks on how "it seemed that I had to choose between two facts, to decide which of them was true, to such an extent was the fact of Albertine's death . . . in contradiction with all my thoughts of her, my desires, my regrets, my tenderness, my rage, my jealousy."[183] He describes this as a painfully upsetting example of admixture or amalgamation, so remarkable that it qualifies in an important sense as contradictory. How could it even be possible that both Robert de Saint-Loup and Albertine herself, who mentioned Marcel's own illness so often, were now quite bluntly the ones "who were dead,"[184] the ones who had died young? And yet it was not only possible; it was actually the case. What is so moving about these untimely deaths is their sheer contingency, their unlikelihood.

There is also the perplexing "mix" between knowing and unknowing, endemic to the project of *partially* apprehending other minds. This is especially pronounced in a person who "liked to fix my thoughts only upon what was still obscure to me," such as Marcel.[185] "As soon as she had suspected that I was in love with

---

The Basic Problems of Phenomenology, revised edition, trans. Albert Hofstadter (Bloomington: Indiana University Press, 1982), 171–173.

[183] *The Fugitive*, III: 498–499; see Merleau-Ponty, *Phenomenology of Perception*, 98: "The phantom arm is not a recollection," since it is felt as present *now* (like the haunted wall at the Grand Hotel). On the "contradiction between memory and nonexistence," see *Cities of the Plain*, II: 796.

[184] *Time Regained*, III: 879.

[185] *The Captive*, III: 501, in which this is noted even of the narrator's taste in piano music.

her," Albertine "had divined the existence in me of an inquisitorial sentiment that desires to know, yet suffers from knowing, and seeks to learn still more."[186] This admixture of knowledge and ignorance chronically afflicts Proust's narrator, who is drawn to the "unknown" and "inaccessible" quality of Albertine and her friends to such a degree that Gisèle is attractive *because* she is mysterious whereas Andrée, striking though she is, seems "too much like myself" to be nearly so captivating as Albertine.[187] Insofar as "we love only what we do not wholly possess," the very otherness of the beloved can serve as a condition of our loving her, yet also a torment by virtue of her remaining imperfectly known. To avoid the "painful anxiety" of wondering and speculating about Albertine, Marcel would need to "cease from loving," which he is not about to do as long as the mystery has continued to persist. If love is a hopeless desire to know completely, then our own capacity for loving would need to be subdued for us to attain *ataraxia*. Like other expressions of "the search for truth," Badiou claims, love is "the source of violent existential crises."[188]

Might it be, as Sextus Empiricus suggests, that people whose eyes are bloodshot see everything as tinted red?[189] Although this is not one of his more convincing examples, it does indicate a further reason for skepticism about how things appear. Perhaps the Pyrrhonian skeptic is unfamiliar with the experience of looking through knowingly bloodshot eyes and speculates from without that it *seems* as if they could cause tarnished vision. In doing so, he inadvertently gives further reason for suspending judgment, namely the opacity of other minds:

---

[186] *The Captive*, III: 67.
[187] *Within a Budding Grove*, I: 851–855, 947–949, and 1006. What follows is from *The Captive*, III: 101–102. On the "force" that "exalted cities and women to such a height so long as I did not know them," see *The Captive*, III: 169–170.
[188] Alain Badiou, *In Praise of Love*, trans. Peter Bush (London: Serpent's Tail, 2012), 51–52.
[189] *Outlines of Pyrrhonism*, 1.126.

What good would it have done if I had spoken to Gilberte? She would not have heard me. We imagine always when we speak that it is our own ears, our own mind, that are listening. My words would have come to her only in a distorted form, as though they had to pass through the moving curtain of a waterfall before they reached my beloved, unrecognizable, sounding false and absurd, having no longer any kind of meaning.[190]

Just as the narrator can walk toward the same destination one evening after another, occupied with thoughts of the same woman, without being in any significant manner "in the same state of mind" each time, what he says to Gilberte has to be heard through *her* mind,[191] as if passing through an obscuring medium. The very fact of otherness prevents his meaning from being transparently communicated.

vii.

While she sleeps, Albertine keeps moving in ways that rearrange her features, each time appearing to be "a different woman, often one whose existence I had never suspected," such that Marcel is faced with not one but "countless" Albertines.[192] Every new arrangement reveals another "facet of her personality," some fairly chaste, others seeming to promise "something more spicy," and these contrasting aspects make Proust's narrator unsure about her real nature, as with the skeptic's mode of suspending judgment due to the "constitution" of things: "In herself was she one more than

---

[190] *Within a Budding Grove*, I: 659.
[191] See *The Guermantes Way*, II: 119, a point at which it is the Duchesse de Guermantes with whom Marcel is obsessed.
[192] *The Captive*, III: 66. On Albertine's numerous aspects or manifestations, see *The Captive*, III: 59 and *The Fugitive*, III: 699. The seventh mode of suspending judgment is outlined in Sextus Empiricus, *Outlines of Pyrrhonism*, 1.129–134. Hankinson characterizes it as "something of a rag-bag" category: *The Sceptics*, 176–177.

the other? Perhaps not, but capable of yielding to any number of different possibilities." A specific person such as Albertine is not "a thing with one definite aspect," for there are a "hundred other things which it may equally well be."[193] Nothing else can induce a feeling of radical perplexity about his surroundings quite as readily as her transformations.

Each appearance of Albertine is correlated with a perspective, of course, as she shifts in relation to Marcel's angle of vision; and he is sometimes perfectly willing to declare that "subjective truth" is what ought to concern him above all.[194] That our narrator has such "an anxious need to be tyrannical" in "matters of love" may, for example, be a more noteworthy and interesting fact than whether his jealousies are justified by any of Albertine's actions. He sounds unperturbed in conceding as much, for instance when he observes:

> Certain philosophers assert that the external world does not exist, and that it is within ourselves that we develop our lives. However that may be, love, even in its humblest beginnings, is a striking example of how little reality means to us.[195]

Although at times Marcel is content to accept this, along with the associated belief that, with one's beloved, "her person itself counts for little or nothing," as "what is almost everything is the series of emotions and anxieties which chance occurrences have made us feel in connection with her,"[196] he is at other times discontented

---

[193] *The Guermantes Way*, II: 378–379. Cf. Bersani, *Marcel Proust*, 9–10, on the need "to reduce the world entirely to the images the self already possesses."

[194] *The Captive*, III: 354–355. The *locus classicus* for the existential theme of "subjective truth" is Kierkegaard's pseudonymous *Concluding Unscientific Postscript*, trans. Alastair Hannay (Cambridge: Cambridge University Press, 2009), esp. 159–251.

[195] *The Fugitive*, III: 577. Marcel's thesis that "everything is in the mind" is proposed, e.g., in *Time Regained*, III: 950.

[196] *The Fugitive*, III: 439. Cf. Landy, *Philosophy as Fiction*, 51, on the possibility that "our individual perspective" is "far more interesting than any aspect of external reality, however accurately grasped." This is consistent with such thoughts as that "a certain similarity exists" in "all the women we successively love," due to "the fixity of our own temperament." *Within a Budding Grove*, I: 955.

by the very same supposition. This is the case when he defines the human being as "the creature who cannot escape from himself, who knows other people only in himself," and who, if "he asserts the contrary," is lying.[197]

As noted earlier, when the lover tries to apprehend the beloved, he can do so only as he himself is *at time X*, perceiving her as she is at that same time, *from angle Y*, and so forth. The idiosyncrasies of the lover's subjective disposition might explain why it seems at times as if the lovable qualities of the beloved object are not "verifiable by others," as Swann finds is true of what he comes to see in Odette.[198] Yet we should not forget that one's angle of vision, quite literally, is also a relevant factor. Seen in profile from a theater seat when she is on stage, Rachel has a dignified beauty that can make a person eager to meet her; when one is right in front of her, however, what is most striking is the "milky way of freckles" that pose a distraction.[199] And what is at issue here is not superficial attractiveness merely: it is an intimation of the mind behind the appearances, the one "who set all this outward show in motion." The mystery of individuality, which is both unknowable and the stimulus for our desire to know the other, can seem different as our contingent location alters.

But we cannot ascertain the truth about someone just by shifting from one vantage point to another, because none of them have authority to prevail over how things appear from all other angles. Where does this leave us? With the discovery that "it can only be after one has recognized, not without some tentative stumblings, the optical errors of one's first impression" that one can "arrive at an exact knowledge" by adjusting one's standpoint, "supposing such knowledge to be ever possible." However, "it is not; for while our

---

[197] *The Fugitive*, III: 459.
[198] See *Swann's Way*, I: 258.
[199] *The Guermantes Way*, II: 177–178. Cf. Descombes, *Proust: Philosophy of the Novel*, 268. This fits with the type of examples provided by Sextus Empiricus in *Outlines of Pyrrhonism*, 1.130. Regarding what follows, see *The Guermantes Way*, II: 60.

original impression of him undergoes correction, the person himself, not being an inanimate object, changes."[200] Furthermore, what provokes our curiosity hovers beyond or behind the surface that makes an initial impression on us, prompting us to want to know more. Marcel can reach toward a sleeping Albertine and adjust her facial expression slightly, but he does not thereby possess her, as she "inwardly reached to infinity."[201] This is why, as Sartre notes, "through her consciousness Albertine escapes Marcel even when he is at her side,"[202] aware of precisely where she is and in control of her whereabouts. As she sleeps in his own home, he vainly attempts "to guess what was concealed in her,"[203] observing that even when held in his arms, she escapes him.

Throughout *The Captive* and *The Fugitive*, Proust's hero undergoes an oscillation between longing for what is absent and then failing to value it when it is abundantly there. He wants to visit other places, and to pursue other women, when Albertine is too regularly with him in Paris; yet once she has departed, Marcel loses interest in travel and longs only to bring her back.[204] This is an echo of how, much earlier, he yearned for an introduction to Albertine and her friends right up until the point when it seemed imminent. He resembles the skeptic in recognizing that too much of a good thing can be harmful, even if it seems precious when missing. Left with no way to adjudicate between these affective impressions of greater and lesser significance, Marcel ends up allowing each to cast doubt on its opposite, concluding once again that it is difficult to know the truth in this world. While he may not be like an atheist

---

[200] *Within a Budding Grove*, I: 934. On the way that "the beauty of images is situated in front of things, that of ideas behind them," see *Time Regained*, III: 974.
[201] *The Captive*, III: 393.
[202] Sartre, *Being and Nothingness*, 478.
[203] *The Captive*, III: 370. See also III: 89, where he admits that "I should have liked, not to tear off her dress to see her body, but through her body to see and read the whole diary of her memories and her future passionate assignations."
[204] On his longing to visit Venice see, e.g., *The Captive*, III: 21, 81, 104, 167, 174, 286, 336, 399–401, 412, and 421. On the instantaneous disappearance of that longing, when Albertine disappears, see *The Fugitive*, III: 431.

who is committed to unbelief, the plurality of aspects that Albertine reveals incline him "towards agnosticism"[205] about her true nature.

viii.

Relativity is the vexing term used to introduce the eighth mode of suspending judgment, and it has been called "the most important" by virtue of containing "all the rest" of the tropes listed so far:[206] it is, then, a compendium of the ways in which "all things are relative," as Sextus concludes, due to variations in the subject, the variability of the object, or a combination of both. Never ignorant of his role *as* a subject of experience, Proust's hero incessantly keeps theorizing about how, "when I saw an external object, my consciousness that I was seeing it would remain between me and it," and this "prevented me from ever touching its substance directly."[207] He reports having realized "in the garden at Combray . . . that in all perception there exists a barrier as a result of which there is never absolute contact between reality and our intelligence." Perhaps "what we 'discover' in objects is only what we have put there," the "gleam" of our "own projections bouncing back,"[208] as Marcel often worries. Because it troubles him that what we find in things, in others, depends partially on the structure of our own mind, a rejoinder from Kant is relevant: just as "the light dove, cleaving the air in her free flight, and feeling its resistance, might imagine that its flight would be still easier in empty space," so we too can be misled into wishing to

---

[205] *The Guermantes Way*, II: 374–375. That a fertile Nietzschean proliferation of truths might be yielded from the same evidence is a possibility that our hero does not consider here. Cf. Jessica N. Berry, *Nietzsche and the Ancient Skeptical Tradition* (New York: Oxford University Press, 2011), 150–152.

[206] Charlotte L. Stough, *Greek Skepticism: A Study in Epistemology* (Berkeley & Los Angeles: University of California Press, 1969), 74; see Sextus Empiricus, *Outlines of Pyrrhonism*, 1.135–140.

[207] *Swann's Way*, I: 90. What follows is from *Time Regained*, III: 1023.

[208] Landy, *Philosophy as Fiction*, 114. Cf. *Time Regained*, III: 950–951.

meet with "no resistance" at all[209]—but this would be tantamount to ridding ourselves of the mental configuration needed to apprehend anything, as the bird needs the air to gain traction when using its wings.

Quite apart from his tendency to speculate about creatures with radically different perceptual capacities, or human beings with senses other than the ones we actually have,[210] the narrator of *In Search of Lost Time* takes notice of how perception is influenced by the beliefs we hold at any specific instant. Amid the flux of all the "states of consciousness" through which we view a person, a "considerable part" is played by our "belief," for example either that "we shall see her again at any moment" or else that she "will be almost impossible of attainment."[211] There is a kind of believing implicit in perception, Marcel observes, and the "beliefs which we do not perceive ... are no more assimilable to a pure vacuum than is the air that surrounds us," yet they shape our apprehension:[212]

> This was the point to which I invariably had to return, to those beliefs which for most of the time occupy our souls unbeknownst to us, but which for all that are of more importance to our happiness than is the person whom we see, for it is through them that we see him.... In the same way as, in telling a story (though to far greater purpose here), people mention what the weather was like on such and such a day, I ought always to give its name to the belief that reigned over my soul and created its atmosphere on any given day on which I saw Albertine.

---

[209] Immanuel Kant, *Critique of Pure Reason*, trans. Norman Kemp Smith (New York: St. Martin's Press, 1965), A5/B8–9. In relation to how the eye itself is actively involved in vision, see also Nietzsche, *The Gay Science*, § 299.

[210] See, respectively, *The Guermantes Way*, II: 64; *The Fugitive*, III: 699.

[211] *Within a Budding Grove*, I: 916–917. On belief as inherent in perception, see again Husserl, *Analyses Concerning Passive and Active Synthesis*, 64–66.

[212] *The Captive*, III: 145. The following quotation is from *Within a Budding Grove*, I: 1010. Cf. Colombetti, *The Feeling Body*, 77–81. See also Gernot Böhme, *Anmutungen: Über das Atmosphärische* (Ostfildern von Stuttgart: Edition Tertium Arcaden, 1998), 40–48.

The "atmosphere" of his mind, according to this last image, sets the tone for particular emotions to arise in relation to his beloved, and is defined by what he believes. Not just any belief can function in this profound way, lending a specific tone to everything around him, but his convictions about Albertine—as secure in the other room, or as longing to escape—have the power to suffuse his world. Albertine appears, in light of Marcel's vacillating atmosphere of belief, akin to "the dancer whose colors, form, character, are transmuted according to the endlessly varied play of a projected limelight," so different in herself as to transform Marcel into "a different person, according to the particular Albertine to whom my thoughts had turned; a jealous, an indifferent, a voluptuous, a melancholy" one,[213] each of which was correlated with an emotional atmosphere of its own.

However, even a false belief can lead to a "deluge of reality" and a "cruel stab" of "truth," as when Albertine pretends to know two women whose romantic affair Marcel has witnessed.[214] What is revealed to our narrator by virtue of his misconception is a fact he had not realized, about how strongly he wants to keep Albertine with himself only. Because, in Proust's world, "two birds in the bush" are always of "greater value than one in the hand,"[215] Albertine's importance to Marcel becomes clear when he fears losing her, in the same manner that her beauty and that of her friends is made apparent to him the minute when he discerns that a long-coveted opportunity to meet them has just been foolishly missed. At the same time, insofar as "the idea of the person we love is reflected in the light of an intelligence that is on the whole optimistic," our hopeful beliefs may also disclose features of the beloved that an indifferent observer would miss.[216] While "there is a certain objective reality"

---

[213] *Within a Budding Grove*, I: 1009–1010.
[214] See *Cities of the Plain*, II: 1151–1154.
[215] Beckett, *Proust*, 16.
[216] *Within a Budding Grove*, I: 675. Regarding a lover's need "to find reasons for his passion," by recognizing in the beloved "qualities which . . . are worthy of love," see *Swann's Way*, I: 444. Love's "friendly eye" is defended persuasively by Jollimore in *Love's*

to people, as Marcel admits, for those who are *not* in love he asks, "is there any need to know a fact?"[217] As he acknowledges, one is not "a very good judge" about matters in which one takes no interest whatever. An affectively charged consciousness may be partial, but a purely neutral attunement is obtuse.

During an unhappy period during which Swann "was always in that tremulous condition which precedes the onset of tears," this emotional disposition orients him toward certain truths, such as all the signs that Odette's attitude toward him is not what it was when she loved and adored him.[218] When he feels jealous toward the self she used to love, and toward Forcheville as a rival for her attention, he scarcely exemplifies the "just and loving gaze" described earlier, an "intense affirmation of another being, irrespective of his attitude toward us," though he does not view her *only* through the lens of jealousy either.[219] Her smile, which was once so affectionately friendly that it won him over, still seems beautiful to him. He cherishes everything "Odette's person," her presence, has made him feel—and he is saddened by the tragic fact that Odette's love for him, and his for her, coexisted for such a brief time. From a dispassionate standpoint, Swann would have remained blind to Odette's allure *and* invulnerable to the torments she induces. Lest we reject jealousy as a misleading influence, we must remember that in Proust's novel jealous opinions tend to be confirmed. There is little basis for calling them a *barrier* to reality, unless they utterly obfuscate

---

Vision, 53 and 62–64. See also Kamila Pacovská, "Love and the Pitfall of Moralism," *Philosophy* 93 (2018): 231–249.

[217] I quote from *The Guermantes Way*, II: 590–591; then, *The Captive*, III: 92. The following reference is to *Within a Budding Grove*, I: 676, where Marcel says, "One is not very particular, nor a very good judge, about things which no longer matter to one."

[218] See *Swann's Way*, I: 372.

[219] Again, see Murdoch, *Existentialists and Mystics*, 327–329. See also Ortega, *On Love*, 44. Regarding the example that follows, see *Swann's Way*, I: 331 and see also Nehamas, *Only a Promise of Happiness*, 56–57: Odette and Swann "were hardly ever in love at the same time," yet when they were "they had both been willing to let the other's desires give shape to their own."

any redeeming qualities in the beloved—which, in Swann's case regarding Odette, they obviously do not.

Bersani posits that "indifference toward others is a state in which we are unresponsive to what is lovable" in them,[220] and for this reason *not* a state to which epistemic privilege ought to be granted. Because he views Odette with loving eyes, Swann is delighted by her habits of speech, "just as if he had been in love with a Breton girl, he would have enjoyed seeing her in her coif and hearing her say that she believed in ghosts."[221] He illustrates Marcel's contention that a "clear perception" of certain imperfections "in those we love" leads us, by virtue of our affection, to regard the traits as "charming,"[222] as the narrator's grandmother manifests through her fondness for what he himself characterizes as his "defects." Even Marcel notes that a person who loves should not be concerned about how the beloved appears to someone else "who does not love her," indeed should not care "what anyone else than the lover himself may think," although these remarks are intermixed with claims that a person's need "to find reasons for his passion" may lead to skewed judgments based on "a difference in optics" that confounds our sense of the beloved's "insignificance or gravity," relatively speaking.[223] His inclination here is not to wish for a standpoint free of bias, though, but just to be uncertain about how to justify the lover's attunement. He is not conflating knowledge with indifference or, in Nietzsche's terms, idealizing "an eye ... in which the active and interpretive forces ... are to be absent," offering us the philosopher's fiction of a completely unbiased point of view.[224]

---

[220] Bersani, *Marcel Proust: The Fictions of Life and of Art*, 190.
[221] *Swann's Way*, I: 268–269. If we are amused by Swann's attempt to persuade himself that the Verdurins have "a more profound comprehension of existence than all your text-books of philosophy," this is because we know he is making excuses for going where Odette is apt to be found. See *Swann's Way*, I: 272.
[222] See *Within a Budding Grove*, I: 663; see also *Cities of the Plain*, II: 785.
[223] I cite *The Fugitive*, III: 447 and then *Swann's Way*, I: 444.
[224] Friedrich Nietzsche, *On the Genealogy of Morality*, trans. Maudemarie Clark and Alan J. Swensen (Indianapolis: Hackett Publishing Company, 1998), Third Essay, § 12.

Such an indefinite "eye" would lack the focus required to see anything whatsoever.

For all the narrator's attestations to the contrary, the world of others is not his own projection, but capable of impressing him in dangerously surprising ways. His first glimpse of Albertine *looking at him* makes him wish to "possess" the intriguing "unknown world" she embodies, behind the eyes that he knows are *not* stones of opal, agate, or mica.[225] That Marcel speaks of possessing the beloved brings to mind associations of ownership and control. Nevertheless, to possess her can also indicate having more of the unknown world of her subjectivity in one's life, by *knowing* it more fully. What he sees in Albertine's gaze is the singular reality of another subject, one that he will wish to know better as long as he continues to be drawn toward her: "In her heart of hearts what was she? What were her thoughts? What were her loves?"[226] He refers also to the "occult forces" that she harbors, the seemingly magical properties that attract him to her and which he can barely account for. And the more Proust's narrator learns, the more he feels that further mysteries remain, that what eludes him is "that unknowable thing which, when we seek to form a definite idea of it, another person's life invariably is to us."[227] If he feels that he is unable to find anything new in Albertine, this can only be a sign of his indifference, because when he is in love she seems inexhaustible to him. He concludes that "the unknown element in the lives of other people is like that of nature, which each fresh scientific discovery merely reduces but does not abolish."[228]

---

[225] *Within a Budding Grove*, I: 851–853. He revisits this disanalogy in *The Captive*, III: 169. Cf. Bowie, *Proust Among the Stars*, 15. (New York: Columbia University Press, 1998)

[226] *The Fugitive*, III: 527. Regarding what follows, see *Cities of the Plain*, II: 1165; see also *Within a Budding Grove*, I: 539–540.

[227] *The Captive*, III: 56. On the "essential quality" of another subject's world, "into which love for another person does not allow us to penetrate," but that a musical composition (for instance) can hint at, see *The Captive*, III: 156.

[228] *The Captive*, III: 398–399. Cf. *The Fugitive*, III: 425.

In an earlier chapter, I made note of Landy's remark that, "As long as [Proust's narrator] is attached to Albertine, he is too close to see her clearly; once his jealousy has abated, he no longer cares enough to try."[229] This captures well a dilemma that troubles Marcel, although some of his protestations of unconcern might be explained as examples of him taking her presence for granted. When he says, "I was bored" with Albertine, or that he finds her "even more boring,"[230] such claims are made first in the context of knowing her exact whereabouts, then after hearing that the chauffeur whom he sent to follow her has nothing interesting to report. Marcel is not a reliable authority about the state of his emotional a priori disposition when he denies loving or caring about Albertine even as he remains "preoccupied with the way in which she disposed of her time," for it is his underlying care that renders intelligible his jealous attention; and he continues experiencing feelings of anxiety "lest Albertine should leave me" and then relative calm when he believes that she will stay.[231] Only a while after her demise does Marcel experience the death of his earlier self who loved her, after a gradual process which can be named "becom[ing] another person" or, alternately, "chang[ing] the face of the world."[232] Near the very end of the narrative, he regards it as a kind of enigma that at each moment of life "we are surrounded by things and people which once were endowed with a rich emotional significance that they no longer possess,"[233] a significance whose relativity may be compatible with its palpable reality.

This returns us to the thought that, when we do find significance or meaning in aspects of the world, our subjective outlook is playing an active role in disclosing the meaning we perceive. That,

---

[229] Landy, *Philosophy as Fiction*, 89.
[230] *The Captive*, III: 4 and 130.
[231] *The Captive*, III: 14 and 408–409. That his life with her fluctuates between boredom and painful jealousy is evident to Marcel: see *The Captive*, III: 400.
[232] *The Fugitive*, III: 656–657.
[233] *Time Regained*, III: 1086.

102 LOVE, SUBJECTIVITY, AND TRUTH

according to some existential phenomenologists, demonstrates how the person and his or her concrete surroundings are mutually interdetermined, neither of them being specifiable without reference to the other.[234] Yet if indeed "loving helps us to discern," as Proust's narrator at one point claims,[235] then our particular affective standpoint must be capable of revealing something true about the world. Or, to put it differently, Marcel's tenacious wish "to understand Albertine's true state of mind" cannot be the mere byproduct of a desire to predict her actions;[236] it must be, rather, that he cares what she does due to a deeper emotional orientation, a love that seeks by its very nature to know *this* other being. And she must have a beauty which, if not self-evident to the cold glance of an "indifferent onlooker,"[237] can be apprehended through the imaginative receptivity of a loving subject.

When this happens, it is not simply "as if a magic lantern threw the nerves in patterns on a screen," objectifying an inner state much in the way that the character Golo is projected around the room by the youthful Marcel's magic lantern,[238] forcing wall, curtains, and doorknob to lose their own nature and be changed into the embodiments of Golo instead. The interplay of a receptive subject and a world that pushes back allows Marcel's fascination with Gilberte and Albertine to show his own affective style *as well as* characteristic features of the two women, which we should have no trouble distinguishing from each other. Upon the vanishing

---

[234] Once again, see Scheler, *Formalism in Ethics and Non-Formal Ethics of Values*, 393–395. See also Solomon, *True to Our Feelings*, 55–56.

[235] *Within a Budding Grove*, I: 969. On the difference of a finite perspective, and the concept of truth which can make room for this, see Rawlinson, "Art and Truth: Reading Proust," 2. See also Gérard Bensussan, *L'Écriture de l'involuntaire: Philosophie de Proust* (Paris: Classiques Garnier, 2020), 125.

[236] See, e.g., *The Captive*, III: 367.

[237] *The Fugitive*, III: 446–447.

[238] From line 105 of "The Love Song of J. Alfred Prufrock," in T. S. Eliot, *Selected Poems* (San Diego: Harcourt Brace Jovanovich, 1934), 11–16, 15. On Golo and the "magic lantern" in Proust, see *Swann's Way*, I: 9–11; see also Bersani, *Marcel Proust: The Fictions of Life and of Art*, 233–236.

of Albertine, Proust's narrator feels the shock of learning things about her *and* about himself.[239] What she affords him is the opportunity to find himself *in* discovering the world. Whereas "throughout the whole course of one's life, one's egoism sees before it all the time the objects that are of concern to the self," far more difficult is taking account of "that 'I' itself which is incessantly observing them."[240] So although he is skeptical toward his emotional impressions because of their relativity, he realizes that the vantage point from which he doubts them is also relative and not absolute. An existential lesson that (arguably) he eventually learns is that, since we lack a view from nowhere, in order "to see we must stand somewhere and trust that our perspective, including our emotional 'take' on the world, finite and limited as it is, is one that enables us to see something."[241] Our subjective viewpoint might actually enable us to apprehend what is true. In other words: no *Dasein*, no truth;[242] yet even though "the appearance of the sensory world at a given time may be relative to a person's emotional commitments at that time," this can be met with either skepticism or trust regarding how things seem. Scheler would say that only in an age of extreme "confusion of hearts" or "*désordre du coeur*" would we find it plausible to doubt the reality of the values that are emotionally disclosed to us.[243]

---

[239] Ronald de Sousa calls emotions "Janus-faced" for their capacity to reveal both subject and object. *Emotional Truth* (Oxford: Oxford University Press, 2011), 69–70. Cf. Nussbaum, *Love's Knowledge*, 261–268. See also Bersani, *Marcel Proust*, 113–117. Regarding what follows, see *The Fugitive*, III: 568; *The Captive*, III: 126–127.

[240] *The Fugitive*, III: 474–475. On skepticism as a refusal of human finitude, a protest against our condition, see Stanley Cavell, *In Quest of the Ordinary* (Chicago: University of Chicago Press, 1988), 5–6 and 88–89.

[241] C. Stephen Evans, *Kierkegaard* (Cambridge: Cambridge University Press, 2009), 64. I am in agreement with Evans that this is a characteristically Kierkegaardian idea.

[242] Heidegger, *Being and Time*, §§ 44(c) and 63; see also Manfred S. Frings, *Max Scheler* (Pittsburgh: Duquesne University Press, 1965), 203–204. What follows is quoted from Mark R. Wynn, *Renewing the Senses* (Oxford: Oxford University Press, 2013), 57.

[243] Scheler, *Formalism in Ethics and Non-Formal Ethics of Values*, 259–262.

ix.

We have seen ample evidence of the Proustian law which stipulates that "one loves nothing but the absent."[244] This general rule can take a form that links it with the ninth skeptical mode, having to do with how frequent or rare a phenomenon is. The sun, if it were only seldom visible, would seem to us "much more amazing than a comet," yet because it is more commonly seen we are actually less amazed by it.[245] Sextus, inviting us to share this intuition, pursues the example further: what if the sun rose ever so rarely, bathing everything in bright light for only a moment before disappearing again? Would this not strike us as more astonishing than smaller and dimmer celestial events that command our attention due only to the rarity of their occurrence? We tend to undervalue what we are accustomed to perceiving, for no other reason than because it is regularly there. Accordingly, Marcel notices that a person can present us with "a dreary face" if we believe he or she is "at our perpetual disposal," a more attractive face when he or she is evading us; and he vows to "grasp a little more closely the nature of this force ... which exalted cities and women to such a height so long as I did not know them," but made them commonplace when close at hand.[246] In this manner, Albertine is transformed from a bland captive to a marvelous, exotic being when she moves far away, leaving Marcel unsure of which impression to trust. Physical distance is what makes her cease to be accessible, and hence to seem rare and precious.

He admits to being inattentive to his dearly beloved grandmother while he is obsessed with finding another opportunity to meet the

---

[244] Again, see Merleau-Ponty, *Institution and Passivity*, 37.
[245] Sextus Empiricus, *Outlines of Pyrrhonism*, 1.141ff.
[246] *The Captive*, III: 179 and 169–170. See also *The Captive*, III: 138–139, on the difference "between a woman glimpsed and [one] approached and caressed." Cf. *The Fugitive*, III: 481, on Albertine seeming more attractive again after she is absent from his daily life, located in a place where he will seldom (if ever) see her again.

band of girls whom he has barely glimpsed and who may (as far as he knows) be leaving Balbec at any moment, just as he once longed so much to be in Gilberte's company that his grandmother's well-being mattered as an instrumental good only,[247] enabling him to visit the Champs-Elysées or preventing him from doing so and thus from having a chance to meet his beloved friend. These other attachments mean more to him at present because the loved others are not constantly available in the same way that his grandmother currently is. However, when he contemplates the possibility of being without her for a while, then faces the reality of her death,[248] he finds their separation unbearable and wants nothing so much as to "stay with her throughout eternity." Giving authority to experiences in which a person's company seems valuable to Proust's narrator, one could argue that these provide him with insights which ought to be taken seriously at other times. It tells him something when he finds attractive the contrafactual possibility, "if Albertine had been alive, how delightful it would have been, on the evenings when I had dined out, to arrange to meet her out of doors, under the arcades!"[249] He imagines her advancing toward him, with "her smiling eyes which had already seen me," and how they would walk along with their arms around each other. A date with Albertine, a conversation with her, are now as rare as a sun that has permanently set, but that he remembers as having been brilliant. To say that it is all too easy for Marcel to appreciate her now that she is gone would be to neglect what a painful longing he experiences. Among all the "perspectives and affective interpretations" which are "useful for knowledge,"[250] in Nietzsche's terms, we ought to

---

[247] See *Within a Budding Grove*, I: 890–891; see also *Swann's Way*, I: 433.
[248] *Within a Budding Grove*, I: 781–782; *Cities of the Plain*, II: 786–790.
[249] *Time Regained*, III: 756–757. Cf. *The Fugitive*, III: 503–504. In such moments, we note that he does not have a generic wish to meet with *someone*.
[250] Again, see Nietzsche, *On the Genealogy of Morality*, Third Essay, § 12. See also Christopher Janaway, *Beyond Selflessness* (Oxford: Oxford University Press, 2007), 210: "Our feeling shocked, embarrassed, disgusted, or attracted by some phenomenon *tells us something about* that phenomenon."

include the emotional distress felt by our narrator when he misses Albertine and wishes she were with him.

"Moral uncertainty," Marcel claims, "is a greater obstacle to an exact visual perception than any defect of vision would be,"[251] and one of his main uncertainties about Albertine is whether or not she wants to leave him. Even the thought of her potentially departing makes his heart race: "I felt untold anxieties which I could scarcely contain rise up in me as in a gust of wind. The tumult in my chest was so great that I was out of breath, as if buffeted by a storm." A moment later, reassured by Françoise that Albertine is right at home in her room, he becomes visibly calmer and tries to persuade himself that it was absurd to be so upset by the possibility. "I breathed again; my agitation subsided; Albertine was here; it was almost a matter of indifference to me whether she was or not. Besides, had it not been absurd of me to suppose that she could possibly not be there?"[252] He professes indifference, but Marcel's agitation betrays him: he does *not* feel that Albertine's availability is an indifferent matter, and he does *not* know for sure if she is there or elsewhere. In relation to others, he is able to notice how much can be wordlessly revealed by signals of emotion such as "a rush of blood to the cheeks of a person who is embarrassed,"[253] but he only inadvertently lets us know what his own emotional agitation reveals.

Five years earlier, Proust's hero says, he would have been "quite indifferent" to all that could now elicit "so intense an anguish," all that Albertine may have done, her body "stretched out to the infinity of all the points that it had occupied in space and time";[254]

---

[251] Again, see *The Captive*, III: 136. This statement could imply that language "enters into the very fabric of one's perceptual experience." Eliot Deutsch, *Creative Being: The Crafting of Person and World* (Honolulu, HI: University of Hawaii Press, 1992), 20.

[252] *The Captive*, III: 410.

[253] *The Captive*, III: 83. On visible passionate agitation, see Scheler, *The Nature of Sympathy*, 260 and Dan Zahavi, *Self and Other* (Oxford: Oxford University Press, 2014), 117–120. Cf. Colombetti, *The Feeling Body*, 176–177 and Joel Krueger, "Empathy and the Extended Mind," *Zygon* 44 (2009): 675–698.

[254] *The Captive*, III: 366–367; then, James, *The Varieties of Religious Experience*, 140. Regarding what follows, see once again *Swann's Way*, I: 450.

this bears on what has been called "notorious," that "the same fact will inspire entirely different feelings," not only in different people, but indeed "at different times in the same person." Five years ago, without the "supplementary sense" that love provides, he would not have perceived "an indefinable quality analogous in the world of the emotions to what in the world of colors is called infra-red" about Albertine. His jealous obsession with her other loves, past, present, and future, does make him attend exceedingly to certain aspects of Albertine; yet it does not prevent him from also being receptive to other features of her distinct being. She is, as Marcel concedes with tongue in cheek, "not wholly invented," but capable of making him "startled" time after time by "a new facet of her personality."[255] Just as surely as the mole on her face resides not on her cheek or chin but above her upper lip, she has her own distinguishing traits which are not of anyone else's invention.[256] Albertine enjoys riding her bicycle even in the rain, loves to imagine dinners made from all the fresh foods called out by street vendors in the city, has a seductive voice, hums popular songs around the house, is capable of great tenderness, and forms her own opinions about such matters as politics and poetry.[257] She is also elusive, enigmatic, in her own way. Proust's narrator, despite himself perhaps, does bring to light aspects of her individuality.[258] Love is not (only) a kind of blindness, but (also) an opening to what is other than oneself. Marcel's horizons are widened by his having taken an interest in Albertine.

Therefore, *In Search of Lost Time* gives the lie to the idea that we can take at face value all of its narrator's statements about the "subjective nature" of love, as if they represented the view endorsed

---

[255] *The Captive*, III: 59 and 353.
[256] See *Within a Budding Grove*, I: 938. "Her mole, which I had visualized now on her cheek, now on her chin, came to rest for ever on her upper lip, just below her nose."
[257] See, respectively, *Within a Budding Grove*, I: 954; *The Captive*, III: 122–123; *The Guermantes Way*, II: 374; *The Captive*, III: 3; *Cities of the Plain*, II: 1160–1161; *The Captive*, III: 10; and *The Fugitive*, III: 464. See also 116-118 below.
[258] Bersani is almost alone in detecting this: see *Marcel Proust: The Fictions of Life and of Art*, 113. See also Kubala, "Love and Transience in Proust," 547–551.

by its author or by the novel as a whole.[259] If "the tragedy of other people" *were* "that they are merely showcases for the very perishable collections of one's own mind," then it would follow that his love for Albertine was "a mental state," thus "not so much a love for her as a love in myself," as Marcel asserts at a time when this love has begun to fade.[260] "She was very sweet" does *not* reduce without remainder to "I experienced pleasure when I kissed her,"[261] as Marcel ought to know. In our affective experience, the relation of an emotion to what that emotion is *about*—to its intentional object—is different in kind, and experientially feels different, from the relation of my bruise to the blunt object that struck me. A bruise is the effect of a cause,[262] whereas Marcel's love inherently contains a reference to whomever he is in love with.

He admits to "feeling a profound astonishment" every time "some new facet" of Albertine is revealed,[263] echoing an idea expressed about Swann, that he finds a mysterious "charm" in discovering each one of Odette's favorite "plays and pictures and places," because they offer insight into her being.[264] "Individual charm," described as the element we cannot invent, is that "which we can

---

[259] This phrase is used in *Within a Budding Grove*, I: 505; *The Fugitive*, III: 568. See also, e.g., *Swann's Way*, I: 258; *Within a Budding Grove*, I: 917–918; *Cities of the Plain*, II: 1154–1155; and *Time Regained*, III: 950–951.

[260] *The Fugitive*, III: 568. Cf. Nussbaum, *Love's Knowledge*, 271–272, for a critical view. See also Allen Thiher, *Understanding Marcel Proust* (Columbia, SC: University of South Carolina Press, 2013), 229–230: he recaps "Proust's vision of love" as "a subjective state" in which the lover "is facing an opacity on which he projects what he may." On the notion that life is "a wholly subjective affair," in which we pursue "the projections of our own mind," see May, *Proust*, 71. The dangers of assigning a narrator's views to the author are stressed in Landy, *Philosophy as Fiction*, 25; Nora Hämäläinen, *Literature and Moral Theory* (London: Bloomsbury, 2015), 183.

[261] See *Time Regained*, III: 933.

[262] Marcel's mistaken reference to love as the "cause" of a condition internal to the beloved include *The Fugitive*, III: 475; *Swann's Way*, I: 373. In the latter, Swann's love for Odette is compared to a disease caused by a microbe.

[263] Or that of one of her friends, at this moment, although he refers to "the other person" in the singular: *Within a Budding Grove*, I: 977. Landy points out that "surprises prove to us that we have not dreamed the world, that it exceeds our oneiric capacity." *Philosophy as Fiction*, 79.

[264] Here I cite *Swann's Way*, I: 269.

seek from reality alone,"[265] as Marcel also illustrates: "Albertine greatly admired a big bronze I had by Barbedienne," which he had thought unlovely but kept around anyway before she was there; once Albertine developed "a certain respect for the bronze," her appreciation "was reflected back on me in an esteem which, coming from Albertine, mattered infinitely more to me than the question of keeping a bronze which was a trifle degrading, since I loved Albertine."[266] An item he was in the habit of not appreciating because he saw it every day thereby became redeemed, providing an obvious counterexample to the sweeping claim that we can value only what appears at rare intervals. Proust's hero finds that his vision of this object is renewed: the bronze is worthy of being there just because it is loved by *his* beloved.

X.

Talking with the narrator and Saint-Loup, the Baron de Charlus postulates that *whom* we love is unimportant, for what matters is only *that* we love: "What matters in life is not whom or what one loves," but rather "it is the fact of loving."[267] Be that as it may, we are seldom permitted to love whomever we choose. Our beloved might be committed to someone else, even if almost against his or her will; or they might be of the "wrong" gender, ethnicity, or age, according to the societal biases of our time. "Morel is mine," says Charlus, with an air of possessive jealousy, and "this testimony, in the eyes of the world and in his own, pleased M. de Charlus more than anything.[268] Yet the young bisexual violinist, his lover and beloved, is ultimately

---

[265] *Within a Budding Grove*, I: 620.
[266] *The Captive*, III: 174. The "truth" in which Proust believes, writes Roger Shattuck, is attained by "a miracle of vision." See *Proust's Way* (New York: W. W. Norton and Company, 2000), 100.
[267] *Within a Budding Grove*, I: 819.
[268] *The Captive*, III: 44.

not to be his to keep, for "society" will not allow it. Obviously, some societies have *not* stigmatized homosexuality and bisexuality, while others have denounced these orientations, persecuting deviations from the norm in the name of conformity. This brings us to the tenth and final skeptical mode of suspending judgment. It is "mainly concerned with ethics, being based on rules of conduct, habits, laws, legendary beliefs, and dogmatic conceptions," and the ways in which these vary from one human being, or group, or nation, to another.[269]

As my focus is more on the personal aspect of existence than on the socio-political, I will here touch only briefly on a prominent issue in Proust's narrative, namely "the question of how the already thorny issue of male representation of female homosexuality becomes further complicated in the context of a work written by a gay man," and how we should "understand what it means for a gay male author to have accorded such vast importance to his heterosexual male narrator's obsession with lesbianism."[270] More accurately, one might say: with bisexuality, especially but not only in women:

> Had either of them a real feeling for me? And, in themselves, what were Albertine and Andrée? To know the answer, I should have to immobilize you, . . . I should have to cease to love you in order to fix your image, cease to be conscious of your interminable and always disconcerting arrival, O girls, O successive rays in the swirling vortex wherein we throb with emotion on seeing you reappear while barely recognizing you, in the dizzy velocity of light[!] We might perhaps remain unaware of that velocity . . . did not a sexual attraction set us in pursuit of you, O drops of gold, always dissimilar and always surpassing our expectation![271]

---

[269] Sextus Empiricus, *Outlines of Pyrrhonism*, 1.145–163.
[270] Elisabeth Ladenson, *Proust's Lesbianism* (Ithaca, NY: Cornell University Press, 1999), 4–6.
[271] *The Captive*, III: 58–59.

To seek the true nature of another subject in the context of practical life involves a willingness to acknowledge what has been described as the "truth of *praxis*," involving our habitual way of life,[272] our "rules of conduct" in Sextus's terms, the habits and practices that form the Aristotelian basis of character. The anti-skeptic who values truths of this kind might say that failing to accept contextual truth is, in Dewey's words, "a personal shortcoming."[273] Regarding the practical habits that shape our dispositions, he writes, "emotion is the moving and cementing force. It selects what is congruous and dyes what is selected with its color."[274] In other words, habit-shaped experience is pervasively emotional—and this provides the skeptic with grounds for doubt.

Habit, Marcel observes, enables "most of our faculties" to "lie dormant." All it takes is a disruption of our everyday routines, such as when we travel, and suddenly, jostled out of our habits, we find ourselves experiencing the world anew. "My habits . . . for once were missing, and all my faculties came hurrying to take their place, vying with one another in their zeal," heightened to an "unaccustomed level, from the basest to the most exalted, from breath, appetite, [and] the circulation of my blood to receptivity and imagination."[275] Habit is thus a "dread deity," an "annihilating force which suppresses the originality and even the awareness of one's perceptions."[276] The skeptic would ask, are things truly the way they seem in familiarized perception, or when they strike us as new? But the latter itself is more than one way of seeming, as it has not only exhilarating but also frightening potential. Think, for instance, of

---

[272] James D. Reid, *Heidegger's Moral Ontology* (Cambridge: Cambridge University Press, 2019), 84–93. See also Victor Kestenbaum, *The Phenomenological Sense of John Dewey: Habit and Meaning* (Atlantic Highlands, NJ: Humanities Press, 1977), 29–30 and 62: "Without habits which provide taken for granted meanings, there would be no self to be in a situation." Indeed, "habits *are* the self."

[273] John Dewey, *The Quest for Certainty*, ed. Jo Ann Boydston (Carbondale, IL: Southern Illinois University Press, 1988), 189.

[274] John Dewey, *Art as Experience* (New York: Perigee Books, 1980), 42–43.

[275] *Within a Budding Grove*, I: 706.

[276] *The Fugitive*, III: 426.

how Marcel feels when he looks around the hotel room at Balbec for the first time, before he has become accustomed to it. The surrounding furniture possesses a startling novelty that unsettles him. "It is our noticing them that puts things in a room, our growing used to them that takes them away again and clears a space for us. Space there was none for me in my bedroom (mine in name only) at Balbec; it was full of things which did not know me, which flung back at me the distrustful glance I cast at them."[277] Notice how he says that "growing used to" things "takes them away" from us: as the furniture in this room becomes familiar to him, he often fails to notice it consciously at all.

Therefore, it is easy to take for granted how things appear to us during the "familiar, humdrum life" in which we can rest on "the solid ground of habit."[278] Life under one roof with Albertine quickly becomes or *seems* boring, a barrier to Marcel's freedom to travel and to pursue other women; she has become, as it were, another piece of furniture in his daily routine. "Familiarity and repetition dull our senses," as one philosopher writes,[279] whereas awestruck wonder at everyday features of the world depends on a disruption of habit. The taken-for-granted joys of the ordinary are exalted in a pseudonymous work by Kierkegaard, whose emphasis lies on taking comfort in them: "Repetition is the daily bread that satisfies with blessing."[280] When Albertine's presence by his side is something "upon which in fact one is no longer certain that one can rely," even the mere thought of her potential departure gives the narrator "a pang of anguish."[281] To assuage the pain, he tells himself: "I knew

---

[277] *Within a Budding Grove*, I: 717. The theme of a room's furnishings having minds of their own arises as early as *Swann's Way*, I: 4.

[278] *The Captive*, III: 361–362. Cf. Beckett, *Proust*, 20: habit, connected with dullness, is also what reassures us upon awaking that our self still exists.

[279] Clare Carlisle, *On Habit* (London: Routledge, 2014), 2.

[280] Søren Kierkegaard, *Repetition: A Venture in Experimenting Psychology*, trans. Howard V. Hong and Edna H. Hong, in one volume with *Fear and Trembling* (Princeton, NJ: Princeton University Press, 1983), 132.

[281] *The Captive*, III: 362.

quite well that she could not leave me without warning me,"[282] which turns out to be a fateful statement.

According to Cavell, one provocation for "an experience or sense that one may know *nothing* about the real world" is to have been "wrong, in some obvious way, about something you are 'totally convinced' or 'assured' of."[283] Early in her Paris captivity, Marcel believes himself to be quite sure that he is bored with Albertine and no longer in love with her,[284] a conviction that he continually repeats until she has gone. He takes for granted her companionship, and her kisses—"every night, before leaving me, she used to slide her tongue between my lips like a portion of daily bread"[285]—fade into his daily routine, up until the point at which they are taken away, and suddenly seem precious. There are, he realizes, "truths . . . which life communicates to us against our will."[286] When Marcel hears Françoise report that "Albertine has gone," Nussbaum notes, "the anguish occasioned by these words" reveals "the truth of his love," just as "the shock of loss and the attendant welling up of pain show him that his theories were forms of self-deceptive rationalization—not only *false* about his condition but also manifestations and accomplices of a reflex to deny and close off one's vulnerabilities."[287] "I had been mistaken in thinking that I could see clearly into my own heart," Proust's narrator admits. "But now these words, 'Mademoiselle Albertine has gone,' had produced in my heart an anguish such that I felt I could not endure it much longer. So what I had believed to be nothing to me was

---

[282] *The Captive*, III: 406. Marcel is more honest with himself when saying, "I did not believe that she would [leave] the house without telling me, but my unconscious thought so."—*The Captive*, III: 373.
[283] Stanley Cavell, *The Claim of Reason: Wittgenstein, Skepticism, Morality, and Tragedy* (Oxford: Oxford University Press, 1979), 140.
[284] *The Captive*, III: 4. He was not "the least bit in love" with her, he says, protesting too much. See *The Captive*, III: 13. About her, he has "nothing more to learn."—*The Captive*, III: 20.
[285] *The Captive*, III: 2.
[286] *Time Regained*, III: 912.
[287] Nussbaum, *Love's Knowledge*, 263–264.

simply my entire life."[288] And Marcel blames his failure to appreciate what she meant to him on the operation of "Habit." As Sartre notes, "Proust does not limit himself to describing the conclusions which he has been able to make," but rather "he wants to explain these findings."[289] So Marcel surmises that, "when we have arrived at reality, we must, to express it and preserve it, prevent the intrusion of all those extraneous elements which at every moment the gathered speed of habit lays at our feet."[290] The fact that he loved Albertine would seem to be one of the realities that are disclosed by the investigations of Proust's hero.

Skepticism would have us weigh equally the opposed appearances that Albertine is boring and, on the other hand, that she is precious. Does not each of these express "a genuine point of view,"[291] in Proust's language? Perhaps. And yet, if we are concerned with the perspective of an existing individual, there is a practical imperative to choose: the skeptic points out that some cultures practice tattooing and others do not, some have sexual intercourse in public and others do not, and therefore suspends judgment, saying that "we shall not be able to state what character belongs to the object in respect of its real essence."[292] Well and good. But our existential imperative is to choose whether to be tattooed or not, whether Albertine is boring or worth staying with. Nietzsche says that "the properties of things considered in themselves are no concern of ours; we are concerned with them only to the extent that they affect

---

[288] *The Fugitive*, III: 425–426. This last sentence does not appear in French until the Tadié et al. edition, then in subsequent English translations. On "the fraud of habit," see Kierkegaard, *Christian Discourses*, 314–315.

[289] *Being and Nothingness*, 235.

[290] *Time Regained*, III: 934. Despite all this maligning of habit, Proust ought to look favorably on the way that we "live our past" through our habits, and that our "sedimented past" is thus embodied: Kestenbaum, *The Phenomenological Sense of John Dewey: Habit and Meaning*, 34 and 42. On our skillful, habitual orientation in the world, see Merleau-Ponty, *Phenomenology of Perception*, 164–168, 175–177, and 213.

[291] *The Captive*, III: 75.

[292] Sextus Empiricus, *Outlines of Pyrrhonism*, 1.148–149 and 1.163.

us."[293] And what affects us with overwhelming emotion may turn out to be as good an example of truth,[294] or candidate instance of truth, as we are likely to find anywhere.

Skepticism merits being taken more seriously than it often is.[295] One way to interpret what it shows us is that a plurality of vantage points may be revelatory of multifaceted—indeed, sometimes apparently contradictory—truths. However, some of its ways to illustrate this pluralism are not so persuasive as others. Take, for instance, how "the same tower from a distance appears round but from a near point quadrangular,"[296] and ask yourself: might it not be that one mistakenly thought it round, only to *correct* one's first impression on inspecting it at close range? Do we really have equal reason to think it appears round once we find on closer inspection that it has square edges? And what about the ladybug on the outside of the tower, which we can see *at all* only from near at hand? What I am suggesting is that how a beloved person appears to us may have something to do with our attention, which allows us to grasp and apprehend the iridescent features of the one we love—and that, in this respect, those without a loving disposition are condemned to remain in the dark.

---

[293] Friedrich Nietzsche, from his manuscript "The Philosopher," in *Philosophy and Truth: Selections from Nietzsche's Notebooks of the Early 1870's*, trans. Daniel Breazeale (Amherst, NY: Humanity Books, 1979), 37.
[294] Nussbaum, *Love's Knowledge*, 273–274.
[295] Cf. Leo Groarke, *Greek Scepticism: Anti-Realist Trends in Ancient Thought* (Montreal: McGill-Queen's University Press, 1990), 153. Skepticism tends to be "dismissed, not because it has been studied carefully and found wanting, but because it goes against the spirit of Western thought," which "glorifies the use of reason [and] the possibility of science."
[296] Sextus Empiricus, *Outlines of Pyrrhonism* 1.118.

4
On Loving Badly and Discovering Truth Nonetheless

"Love bade me welcome," George Herbert writes, "yet my soul drew back," feeling unworthy. But, then: "Love took my hand, and smiling did reply, / Who made the eyes but I?"[1] Marcel also chastises himself for failing to embody the ideal "just and loving gaze" in his way of seeing Albertine.[2] Being "swayed alternately by trust and by jealous suspicion," he acknowledges that "where I had been wrong was perhaps in not making a greater effort to know Albertine in herself."[3] Viewing himself as an unreliable, emotionally biased epistemic subject, he is genuinely dubious when he asks himself, "could I be certain that I had discovered *anything* about Albertine?"[4]

i.

Leaving aside the issue of certainty, one answer to this query would be the cynical one that he has discovered nothing much. And we find that stance adopted by Nussbaum. She cites a short story (by Ann Beattie) in which we as readers find out (by her count) nine things about the narrator's beloved—and then, perhaps with a

---

[1] George Herbert, "Love (III)," lines 1 and 11–12, in *The Country Parson* [and] *The Temple*, ed. John N. Wall, Jr. (New York: Paulist Press, 1981), 316.
[2] The phrase quoted is from Murdoch, *Existentialists and Mystics*, 327.
[3] Proust, *The Fugitive*, III: 499 and III: 505–506.
[4] *The Fugitive*, III: 665. My emphasis.

Love, Subjectivity, and Truth. Rick Anthony Furtak, Oxford University Press.
© Oxford University Press 2023. DOI: 10.1093/oso/9780197633724.003.0004

conscious bit of hyperbole, Nussbaum asserts that we learn more about this character "in the story's ten pages than about Albertine in three thousand."[5] Is this fair? First of all, Albertine is absent from entire stretches of Proust's narrative, beginning with the times before she has appeared. Taking a merciful view, like "Love" as personified in Herbert's poem, Anne Carson puts forward more generous statistics: she lists at least fifty-nine things we learn about Albertine,[6] and that does not purport to be an exhaustive list. It includes such features as Albertine's frequent habit of napping (as Carson reckons, she is asleep nineteen percent of the time she is named); her bad habit of lying; her bisexuality; her (according to Marcel) charming poor taste in music; "the way the wind billow[s] in her garments" at Balbec; her meager family; the different aspects of her face from the front and in profile; her way of resembling both Proust's chauffeur, Alfred Agostinelli, and the Shakespearean character Ophelia; the geranium scent of her laughter; her hair's resemblance to crinkly black violets; her similarity at Marcel's Paris home to a domestic animal; her way of multiplying into many different Albertines when Marcel kisses her; her favorite stanza by Mallarmé, about a swan frozen into an icy lake; as well as her departure and death. It does not mention anything but the blueness (sometimes described as bluish-green) of her eyes, not that they are bright, laughing, sparkling, brilliant, and smiling; the way she is disposed to sing fashionable music out loud; that, as noted earlier, she is fond of riding her bicycle even in the rain; her skillful piano playing; that she seems to be in the habit of receiving compliments; her delightful trait of always being spontaneously "up for anything"; or her practice of reading aloud to Marcel. List-making can become tedious, but I am sure that we could number Albertine's attributes further, indeed well into the triple digits. Unquestionably, she is a person, a subject in her own right, someone "for whom a

---

[5] Nussbaum, *Love's Knowledge*, 277.
[6] Anne Carson, *The Albertine Workout* (New York: New Directions, 2014), 5–21.

world exists," to use Troy Jollimore's elegant phrase,[7] even as she remains all the time largely unknowable. Nor can Marcel's partial apprehension of Albertine depend upon him succeeding at the Murdochian moral task of getting his "fat relentless ego" out of the way, because he seldom if ever does.[8] The evidence of the novel as a whole outweighs the often-skeptical theoretical statements made by Proust's narrator, suggesting that we can in fact know the world of others.

It is at best an exaggeration to surmise, then, with Landy that "Love [in Proust] . . . subsists on illusion,"[9] or with Beckett that "the person of Albertine counts for nothing."[10] It is the narrator who endorses such claims, but as we have seen he often gets *himself* wrong, saying for instance that Albertine is "utterly meaningless" to him.[11] He is more on target when he concedes that she time and again reveals "a new facet of her personality," and is "capable of yielding to any number of different possibilities in the headlong current of life," just as Odette is, "*simultaneously*, cocotte and fashionable hostess, wife and widow, mother and grandmother, and [at last] newly acquired mistress of the senile Duc de Guermantes."[12] Each woman is multifaceted, having all of the qualities named in Proust along with additional ones. When Marcel is first getting to know Albertine and her friends, he rightly observes that "loving helps [him] to discern, to discriminate" among "the infinite variety of personalities."[13] This is compatible with its being true that, as

---

[7] Jollimore, *Love's Vision*, 90, 125, and 159. Cf. Merleau-Ponty, *Institution and Passivity*, 211: on recovering "the person that we were" when we loved.

[8] Murdoch, *Existentialists and Mystics*, 342. Cf. Simone Weil, "Beauty," in *Simone Weil Reader*, ed. George A. Panichas (Wakefield, RI: Moyer Bell, 1977), 378: "The beautiful is something on which we can fix our attention," but which requires "a renunciation," since "we want to eat all the other objects of desire," whereas "the beautiful is that which we desire without wishing to eat it. We desire [only] that it should be." Cf. Morris Weitz, *Philosophy in Literature* (Detroit: Wayne State University Press, 1963), 86.

[9] Landy, *Philosophy as Fiction*, 11.

[10] Beckett, *Proust*, 37–38.

[11] *The Captive*, III: 21.

[12] *The Captive*, III: 59; Roger Shattuck, *Proust's Binoculars*, 47.

[13] *Within a Budding Grove*, I: 969.

he contends, "people who learn some correct detail about another person's life at once draw conclusions from it which are not accurate,"[14] and that—spoken by a jealous lover—nothing "could be more threatening" to the beloved than the avowal, "I love you," for "it means that one way or another I intend to own you."[15] The famous problem of other minds will never be decisively solved, yet we cannot realistically aspire to transcend our own vantage point and occupy a view from nowhere. Marcel eventually learns this.

ii.

"It is high time," Dietrich von Hildebrand writes, "that we free ourselves from the disastrous equating of objectivity and neutrality." Every "anti-affective trend" in thought, he adds, "fails to conform to the real features and meaning of the cosmos."[16] Marcel is mistaken in concluding that "jealousy [is] powerless to discover anything in the darkness that enshrouds it," and correct when he later recognizes that his "jealousy prevent[s] me from losing sight of Albertine."[17] For he discovers aspects of the world well beyond his own mind even when he is lying in bed in his Paris apartment, at the start of *The Captive*, and detecting what the weather is like by discerning how brightly or dimly the light filters through the curtains, and from what sounds he hears arising from the street below.

---

[14] *The Captive*, III: 1.
[15] William Gass, "Throw the Emptiness Out of Your Arms: Rilke's Doctrine of Nonpossessive Love," in *The Philosophy of (Erotic) Love*, ed. Robert C. Solomon and Kathleen M. Higgins (Lawrence: University Press of Kansas, 1991), 451–466, 457. On Swann's wish "to take [Odette] away from everyone else," see also Sartre, *Being and Nothingness*, 235. Regarding what follows, see Groarke, *Greek Scepticism: Anti-Realist Trends in Ancient Thought*, 74; Genia Schönbaumsfeld, *The Illusion of Doubt* (Oxford: Oxford University Press, 2016), 150–151.
[16] Dietrich von Hildebrand, *The Heart: An Analysis of Human and Divine Affectivity*, trans. John F. Crosby (South Bend, IN: St. Augustine's Press, 2007), 48.
[17] *The Captive*, III: 147 and III: 163. Cf. Milan Kundera, *Farewell Waltz: A Novel*, trans. Aaron Asher (New York: Harper Perennial, 1998), 207–208: "Jealousy is like a raging toothache. One cannot do anything when one is jealous, not even sit down."

Proust's narrator admits that "mental pictures" are easy to form if they do not take actuality into account, and that the beings with whom he becomes obsessed are sometimes only "phantoms, creatures whose reality exist[s] to a great extent in my imagination."[18] But he finds himself, when in love, experiencing an overall intensification of the sense that life is real, so he acknowledges that Madame de Guermantes, for example, has "a real existence independent of myself"—and that, moreover, he is frequently in a position comparable to that of "the idealist philosopher whose body takes account of the external world in the reality of which his intellect declines to believe."[19] He is in a state of bad faith, it is fair to say, when he protests that love is merely subjective.

Referring to Sartre's point that a rocky crag seems "unscalable" only if I desire to climb it, a contemporary existential philosopher comments that this shows "the fundamental ambiguity of situation," as:

> on the one hand, there is no "crag" in the world apart from my (or some other subject's) project of scaling . . . . On the other hand, the "crag" is not explicable solely as a subjective projection of my will and imagination.[20]

Forcheville's affair with Odette is likewise a fact that exists out in the world, beyond the inner confines of Swann's mind, although it has meaning to him by virtue of Swann's love for Odette. Charles Swann is able not only to be "blinded" by jealousy, but also to discern *through* his jealous gaze the threat to his own relationship that Forcheville poses: so it is not only to the detriment of his

---

[18] *The Captive*, III: 15; *Cities of the Plain*, II: 1045.
[19] *Swann's Way*, I: 190–192 and I: 435–436. Cf. May, *Proust*, 26; and, on "subjective idealism," see Landy, *Philosophy as Fiction*, 6.
[20] Ong, *The Art of Being*, 185. See Sartre, *Being and Nothingness*, 620 and 634–635. See also Thiher, *Understanding Marcel Proust*, 144: Proust, he argues, makes a "unique contribution" to "theories of love" by showing how jealousy involves the "anguish felt at the absence of the beloved."

perceptual awareness that Swann goes around in "that tremulous condition which precedes the onset of tears."[21] This is the case despite our being told by Marcel that "our attention in the presence of the beloved" is "too tremulous" for us "to be able to carry away a very clear impression."[22] That is why being deeply curious about Odette is a revival of the same passion for truth "with which he had once studied history." His perspective defines what commands his attention, but it is not within his power to bring about a situation in which Odette is remaining faithful to Swann himself. While "it is true," Merleau-Ponty notes, "that nothing has *significance* and value for anyone but *me* and through anyone but me," this proposition is "indeterminate" as long as "we fail to make clear how we understand significance and the self."[23] We do not have the option of making the unscalable crag into one we could easily climb. So, there are no grounds for epistemic shame in the fact that "the mind eliminates everything that does not concur" with the "element of love" that we bring to all circumstances.[24] In a similar way, Marcel is not being precise when he refers to his fear of Albertine's infidelity as a mere "phobia."[25] Nor is he bestowing onto the world something that is either private or idiosyncratic to himself.

---

[21] *Swann's Way*, I: 410–411 and I: 372. Cf. Calhoun, "Subjectivity and Emotion," 109.

[22] *Within a Budding Grove*, I: 528. See also May, *Proust*, 35. As Bersani notices, Proust "creates characters whose function it is to resist Marcel's fantasies about them."—*Marcel Proust*, 243. With respect to what follows, see *Swann's Way*, I: 298–299.

[23] Merleau-Ponty, *Phenomenology of Perception*, 510–511. On the "sober people" who feel that they are "armed against passion," who "insinuate that the world really is the way it appears" to them, see Nietzsche, *The Gay Science*, § 57.

[24] *Within a Budding Grove*, I: 1012.

[25] *The Captive*, III: 14. Cf. Furtak, *Knowing Emotions*, 54–58. On "the whole marvellous uncertainty and ambiguity of existence," as well as the inevitable idiosyncrasy of each perspective, see Nietzsche, *The Gay Science*, § 2.

iii.

The emotional imagination of the person who loves another may well enable him or her to appreciate actual truths about the beloved, despite the narrator's remark about "how much a human imagination can put behind a little scrap of a face."[26] The attractive appearance of someone whom we love involves our "belief that [he or she] has a share in an unknown life"—it is not just the "changeable elements of flesh and fabric" that come into our view, but what shines through them as if from within, "the invisible person who set[s] all this outward show in motion."[27] So Marcel rhetorically asks: "are they not, those eyes one sees, shot through with a look behind which we do not know what images, memories, expectations, disdains lie concealed?"[28] Other minds beckon to us, inviting us to come to love and to know them, and each of us who accepts this invitation "takes in a certain sphere of fact and trouble" through "his peculiar angle of observation."[29] The heart, then, by virtue of what it embraces and what it rejects, becomes for each of us "the foundation of our personality."[30] We as readers cannot know Albertine as well as we can get to know Anna Karenina, but this is because we can see inside of Anna's mind. This difference could not be more crucial: a Proust with an omniscient narrator ceases to be Proust. Even the grief of Marcel's mother when his grandmother dies is only indirectly glimpsed, through *his* eyes.

Philosophical skepticism can arguably be seen as "an attempt to convert the human condition . . . into an intellectual difficulty, a riddle."[31] There is, as Proust's hero notes, an "essential quality of

---

[26] *The Guermantes Way*, II: 161.
[27] *Swann's Way*, I: 108; *The Guermantes Way*, II: 60.
[28] *The Captive*, III: 167.
[29] James, *The Varieties of Religious Experience*, 436. Cf. Marilyn M. Sachs, *Marcel Proust in the Light of William James* (Lanham, MD: Lexington Books, 2013), 190: "Although we may think we understand the motives and feelings of another person, in fact, they remain . . . a matter almost solely of interpretation. We may try to correct our notions about them but may end up merely substituting one error for another."
[30] Ortega, *On Love*, 79–80.
[31] Cavell, *The Claim of Reason*, 493.

another person's sensations into which love for another person does not allow us to penetrate."[32] And "the mystery of personality" always continues to endure, beyond whatever it is about a person which gets disclosed to us.[33] But this is no reason to shut ourselves off from the vulnerability to which we are exposed in loving. The incomplete knowledge we have of those whom we love is inevitable, and perhaps worthy of Marcel's lamentation when he gives voice to this thought:

> I realized the impossibility which love comes up against. We imagine that it has as its object a being that can be laid down in front of us, enclosed within a body. Alas, it is the extension of that being to all the points in space and time that it has occupied and will occupy.... But we cannot touch all these points.[34]

This, however, hardly justifies our avoidable failures to (love and to) see. In the final chapter, I will assess how we might make the best of our unavoidably limited point of view.

---

[32] *The Captive*, III: 156. On love and vulnerability, see Nussbaum, *Upheavals of Thought*, 313–319; Diane Enns, "Love's Limit," in *Thinking about Love*, ed. Diane Enns and Antonio Calcagno (University Park: Pennsylvania State University Press, 2015), 38–44. Cf. Schönbaumsfeld, *The Illusion of Doubt*, 80: "In fact, 'meaning scepticism' and 'hyper-realism' turn out to be two sides of the same coin: disappointed that nothing will fit the hyper-realist bill... we end up believing that 'meaning scepticism' (or some sort of 'sceptical' solution) is the only available option."

[33] *Swann's Way*, I: 336.

[34] *The Captive*, III: 95. As Robert Pippin observes, jealousy in Proust "is all a function of a general state of unknowingness about the other, a great anxiety, even anguish, that one can never really know who the other is," *Philosophy by Other Means* (Chicago: University of Chicago Press, 2021), 203. See also Jean-Yves Tadié, *Marcel Proust: A Life*, trans. Euan Cameron (New York: Penguin Books, 2000), 204–205: Proust had faith in "Kantian idealism, belief in a 'thing in itself', in a reality hidden behind appearances." On "despair" as the only alternative to pure selfless love, see Sharon Krishek, *Lovers in Essence* (Oxford: Oxford University Press, 2022), 150–190.

5
"Reality as We Have Felt It to Be"

i.

Nietzsche finds it unlikely that words could capture a "single, absolutely individualized original experience," because if we "could perceive now only as a bird, now as a worm, now as a plant,"[1] and so forth, we might think of the world "as a highly subjective construct." Yet he elsewhere provides a sublime formula for affirmation of one's own life in its unique particularity:

> What have you up to now truly loved, what attracted your soul, what dominated it while simultaneously making it happy? Place this series of revered objects before you, and perhaps their nature and their sequence will reveal to you a law, the fundamental law of your authentic self.[2]

One could hardly find a more apt statement of Proust's own existential credo. "Our true life," in the idiom of his narrator, is "reality as we have felt it to be."[3] A view from nowhere would be a

---

[1] "On Truth and Lie in a Nonmoral Sense," trans. Taylor Carman, in *On Truth and Untruth: Selected Writings* (New York: Harper Perennial, 2010), 15–49, 27 and 39. Cf. *The Guermantes Way*, II: 64—"the trees, the sun and the sky would not be the same as what we see if they were apprehended by creatures having eyes differently constituted from ours."

[2] "Schopenhauer as Educator," trans. Richard T. Gray, in *Unfashionable Observations* (Stanford, CA: Stanford University Press, 1995), 169–255, 174.

[3] *Time Regained*, III: 915. On Proust's "perspectivalism," see Rorty, *Contingency, Irony, and Solidarity*, 107. Regarding what follows, see also Schönbaumsfeld, *The Illusion of Doubt*, 152–153: "We desire what is conceptually impossible, because we resent our own finitude." Cf. Thomas Nagel, *The View from Nowhere* (New York: Oxford University

vantage point from which nothing can be discerned at all. Marcel ultimately must come to terms with the pure contingency of his emotional "take" on things. He will always be the young man who feigned indifference, "playing hard to get" as the saying goes, when he first had a chance for Elstir to introduce him to Albertine and her friends, and the one who felt after making their acquaintance that they were "supernatural creatures," as if he "had been playing amid a band of nymphs."[4] The splendidly enchanted world that he experienced one summer at Balbec ends up being vindicated as the only kind of truth he has ever known. When he cannot apprehend the world as beautiful and meaningful, when his infra-red vision is not working, he says that "if ever I thought of myself as a poet, I know now that I am not one,"[5] for "if I really had the soul of an artist, surely I would be feeling pleasure at the sight of this curtain of trees lit by the setting sun, those little flowers on the bank," whose color he cannot "attempt to describe," for, as he asks, "can one hope to transmit to the reader a pleasure that one has not felt?"

The novel overall demonstrates and displays the "whole set of difficulties, ambiguities, and contradictions which constitute the lived meaning of an existence," as Simone de Beauvoir says of modern fiction in general, in which "action, emotion, and feeling" are used in order to evoke "this flesh-and-blood presence" with "complexity and singular and infinite richness."[6] What is personal, singular, about each subject is not "subjective" in a pejorative sense. So we need to reject the suggestion that the world according to Proust is "curiously deformed by his peculiar temperament"

Press, 1986), 108; Reid, *Heidegger's Moral Ontology*, 46: "A gaze cleansed of everything past does not see things as they truly are; it sees precisely—nothing."

[4] *Within a Budding Grove*, I: 914–915; *Within a Budding Grove*, I: 1013.
[5] *Time Regained*, III: 886.
[6] Simone de Beauvoir, "My Experience as a Writer," in *"The Useless Mouths" and Other Literary Writings*, trans. Marybeth Timmermann (Urbana: University of Illinois Press, 2011), 287; "Literature and Metaphysics," trans. Veronique Zaytzeff, in *Philosophical Writings* (Urbana: University of Illinois Press, 2004), 270.

and "his unusual personality."[7] This echoes the scientific bias criticized by Husserl, according to which the goal of "objectivity" requires "the exclusion of everything that is merely subjective" and thus also "ourselves as the functioning subjectivity in whose function the ontic meaning 'world' arises."[8] Meanings proliferate in the Proustian world, giving an overdetermined quality to everything that happens. To capture the impressive nature of a significant world is an artistic task, but also a philosophical one. Philosophy need not strive to transcend the personal "style and idiosyncrasy" of the individual person,[9] but can rather emphasize the particularities of temperament and personality. Every occurrence in life, filtered as it is through the lens of a unique subject, seems "to be governed by magic rather than by rational laws," Marcel says,[10] thinking most of all about unusually luminous moments of insight. As Elstir accomplishes in his paintings, the literary artist manages in Beckett's terms to express "phenomena in the order and exactitude of their perception," revealing "what he sees and not what he knows he ought to see." This, he adds, is the key to Proust's own variety of "impressionism."[11] Our affective impressions determine who we have been and who we are in the process of becoming—and, most crucially, what we *will* have been for all time, that is, our life as a whole.

---

[7] Germaine Brée and Margaret Guiton, *An Age of Fiction* (New Brunswick, NJ: Rutgers University Press, 1957), 55 and 42.

[8] Edmund Husserl, *The Crisis of European Sciences and Transcendental Phenomenology*, trans. David Carr (Evanston, IL: Northwestern University Press, 1970), 256; see also 29, on the misguided goal of overcoming "the relativity of subjective interpretations." Proust's narrator "seeks to combat a prevalent form of materialism with a form of subjective idealism," Jones claims; see *Philosophy and the Novel*, 147. Marcel uses these terms in *Within a Budding Grove*, I: 874.

[9] Alexander Nehamas, *The Art of Living: Socratic Reflections from Plato to Foucault* (Berkeley & Los Angeles: University of California Press, 1998), 3. Cf. Rorty, *Contingency, Irony, and Solidarity*, 25.

[10] Proust, *Within a Budding Grove*, I: 539–540. See also May, *Proust*, 62: "Our authentic glimpses of the world are poetic ones."

[11] Samuel Beckett, *Proust*, 66. Cf. Landy, *Philosophy as Fiction*, 116.

Marcel's outlook or orientation toward the world bears witness to what has moved him most intensely, from the hawthorns in bloom to the death of his grandmother. He owes his very identity to the experience of being emotionally overwhelmed, and he admits candidly that "only from such an impression" could he hope to "extract some truth from life."[12] Even amidst the most profound suffering, he recognizes that one's experience—regardless of how painful it may be—defines the truth about one's singular identity. It allows us to learn who we are via "the truth of our feelings, the truth of our destiny,"[13] accidental and fortuitous though these may be. Our "*affective* finitude," as Ricoeur puts it, takes shape as a "unique, irreplaceable point of view."[14] It constitutes each of our specific personal worlds, the revelation and transcription of which are worthy tasks in their own right.

By being conscious of what one has abidingly loved, one discovers the truth of the self, what one has most intimately known; all that is linked with our history of having loved is animated with the glow of an internal flame. Furthermore, as Marcel reflects, "something solid subsists" after all "vain endeavors," namely "what we love."[15] This is what he calls "felt truth."[16] When we apprehend such a truth, it may not be compatible "with happiness or with physical health,"[17] but our reason for taking it seriously does not depend upon its hedonistic or salubrious merits. It depends only upon what it can teach us about world and self, and, in particular, what is most personally characteristic about these.

---

[12] *Cities of the Plain*, II: 787. This goes against what Levinas argues: "everything I encounter [for Proust] exists as having come out of myself." See *Proper Names*, trans. Michael B. Smith (Stanford, CA: Stanford University Press, 1996), 104.
[13] *The Fugitive*, III: 517. Cf. Badiou, *In Praise of Love*, 40–43.
[14] Ricoeur, *Fallible Man*, 55–56. See also von Hildebrand, *The Heart*, 40. On Marcel's "singular, distinct experiential path," see Pippin, *Philosophy by Other Means*, 180.
[15] *The Guermantes Way*, II: 401. Cf. Nehamas, "Only in the Contemplation of Beauty is Human Life Worth Living," 10: "In the ideal case the various paths we have followed through life on account of the things we have loved ... will gradually transform us too into something that no one has seen before and that is itself worthy of love."
[16] *Time Regained*, III: 926.
[17] *Time Regained*, III: 943.

Realizing that he has lost his beloved grandmother forever makes Marcel's "heart swell to breaking-point," and yet he longs "for the nails that riveted her to my consciousness to be driven yet deeper,"[18] as it is only through this agonizing pain that he knows what has been lost. His felt impression is valued for its truthfulness, because it reveals something meaningful about his life—and not only his own, as he also wonders what the loved one may have felt (for instance, being teased by her grandson for taking a late photograph as a keepsake for him), just as he wonders what Albertine and Andrée feel toward him and how they experience their amorous liaisons with one another and with other women.[19] Because, as Nussbaum remarks, "the cataleptic impressions of love" are the "foundations of all knowledge," a change of heart is bound to threaten the coherence of one's emotional personhood,[20] although if one is lucky it is possible to elicit a narrative arc from even the shifts and changes in one's history of having loved. What begins as an "involuntary history" can be *owned* by being willed, or more gently *accepted*, as one's fate,[21] as the truth of one's existence. And what could very well appear to be "just a disjointed series of events," as one love is followed by another, can take on an overarching shape, "a single emotional tone," as Landy observes.[22]

Proust's narrator confesses to having "an inquisitorial sentiment that ... suffers from knowing, and [yet] seeks to learn still more"; he realizes that this element in him is almost perverse when after her abrupt departure Albertine prompts this series of ideas: "The present calamity was the worst that I had experienced in my life. And yet the suffering that it caused me was perhaps even exceeded

---

[18] *Cities of the Plain*, II: 785–786.
[19] *Within a Budding Grove*, I: 843–844; *The Captive*, III: 58; *The Fugitive*, III: 536–537.
[20] Nussbaum, *Love's Knowledge*, 273. Cf. *Swann's Way*, I: 410; *The Guermantes Way*, II: 404. On changes of heart, see Martin Hägglund, *Dying for Time* (Cambridge, MA: Harvard University Press, 2012), 27–28: Marcel "wants to keep *this* particular life and *these* particular emotions, so the prospect of replacing them with a different life or a different set of emotions is deemed to be unbearable."
[21] Merleau-Ponty, *Institution and Passivity*, 117.
[22] Landy, "Why a Novel?," 28–29.

by my curiosity to learn the causes of this calamity."[23] Trying to "ascertain truth" about Albertine is not as easy as discerning the location of the mole that he imagines himself to have glimpsed on her chin and cheek before identifying that it lies on her upper lip: her being is "difficult to plumb," for she is always changing both in herself and regarding him.[24] Although the project of moving "beyond his own subjectivity" to "enter the consciousness of another human being" never fully succeeds due to Albertine's habit of "always surpassing" his expectations,[25] neither is the project of coming to know her a total failure. Indeed, Marcel has not ceased to learn new things about her even after her death, again notwithstanding the fact that these are mainly painful truths. So the novel enacts the process of bringing into language "what had remained unformulated, obscure, implicit, [or] misapprehended."[26] The proof, in many cases, is in the embodied agitation of an emotional response, as when—just after professing himself "convinced of my indifference to Albertine"—he finds that he is "gripp[ing] my heart in my hands,"[27] which are suddenly moist with sweat upon his being told, "Albertine has gone." The following hundreds of pages after these passages show the great understatement in his admission that "there are things in our hearts to which we do not realize how strongly we are attached,"[28] at least not until the abrupt disappearance of our beloved impinges upon our sensitive, needy, anxious temperament. Just as the beloved other person contains possible worlds yet to be unfolded,[29] our unique life is something that we never possess in its entirety.

[23] *The Captive*, III: 51; *The Fugitive*, III: 433.
[24] *The Captive*, III: 49; *Within a Budding Grove*, I: 938. See also Kubala, "Love and Transience in Proust," 548–549n; *The Captive*, III: 63.
[25] Landy, *Philosophy as Fiction*, 21; *The Captive*, III: 58–59.
[26] Descombes, *Proust: Philosophy of the Novel*, 77 and 241.
[27] *The Captive*, III: 422; *The Fugitive*, III: 425. Cf. Nussbaum, *Love's Knowledge*, 261. See also *Swann's Way*, I: 520.
[28] *The Fugitive*, III: 467.
[29] See, e.g., Deleuze, *Proust and Signs*, 138. With regard to what follows, see Rex Ferguson, "*In Search of Lost Time* and the Attunement of Jealousy," *Philosophy and Literature* 41 (2017): 213–232, 216. What Marcel proffers as universal laws tend to reveal what characterizes his peculiar subjectivity.

Noteworthy is that we can only bring to light what lies hidden in us through our encounter with the external world. We discover our own tendency, if thus it be, to "love a certain type of woman," only upon finding in her "so special a notion of individuality that she seems to us unique in herself and predestined and necessary for us," which is "due to the fixity of our own temperament" above all else.[30] There are, nonetheless, "women whom it was impossible to imagine *a priori*," but ones with whom our contingent paths *did* intersect.[31] Is it not a sort of accident, or a collision of many accidents, that leads Marcel to travel with his grandmother, after all? And Albertine is poorly described as the cause or corollary of Marcel's "pleasure" when he is kissing her;[32] his experience is inextricably linked with someone else, not isolated within his own mind. "One's egoism sees before it all the time the objects that are of concern to the self, but never takes in that 'I' itself which is perpetually observing them,"[33] and so the latter must come to be understood through the refracted light cast by the angle of one's perspective. Our sense of reality is based upon "that ineffable something which differentiates qualitatively what each of us has felt," and we could wish for no greater miracle than "to see the universe through the eyes of another, of a hundred others, to see the hundred universes that each of them sees, that each of them is,"[34] as we as readers do with Marcel. Our distinct individuality is known to us, insofar as it comes to be known at all, only by virtue of our romantic encounter

---

[30] *The Fugitive*, III: 511–512; *Within a Budding Grove*, I: 955.
[31] *The Captive*, III: 20.
[32] *Time Regained*, III: 932–933.
[33] *The Fugitive*, III: 474. See also Landy, *Philosophy as Fiction*, 113–114. Again, consider Thoreau's claim that a person "sees only what concerns him," in "Autumnal Tints," 394.
[34] *The Captive*, III: 257–260. Kristeva remarks on Proust's "affective universe" in *Time and Sense*, 261, tracing this idea to Schopenhauer. See also Jacques Rolland de Renéville, "Thèmes Métaphysiques chez Marcel Proust," *Revue de Métaphysique et de Morale*, 90, no. 2 (1985): 218–229.

with the world of others.[35] As Kierkegaard says, the self is not an inner entity that need only be released from its box in order to spring, fully formed, into being. "Subjective truth," in this sense, arises from engaging with the intersubjective world.[36]

We learn, at a distance, looking at Marcel's subjectivity taking shape, something about how our own is formed. A fiction allows us to "attain a picture of what a particular kind of life may look like," at "a distance impossible to attain regarding one's own life as a whole," as one critic argues.[37] Aesthetic experience thereby makes a valuable contribution to cognitive awareness, and it is anything but disinterested because of how it pertains to our lives. The narrator who "had been mistaken in thinking that I could see clearly into my own heart" finds out through his painful grief upon Albertine's departure that he is, among other things, the person who has loved her.[38] And this insight serves very well his ambition "to have or find or fashion a self,"[39] disclosing the kind of timeless identity that can be formed only via the medium of unfolding temporal sequence. What is at issue for him is not a new bit of knowledge, but instead the meaning of life. This brings Marcel "the joy of rediscovering what is real,"[40] existence as only he has felt it to be. Each turn of the kaleidoscope brings about alterations in the felt quality of our apprehension, and for Proust's hero what ends up emerging and being

---

[35] Cf. Schopenhauer, *The World as Will and Representation, Volume One*, 331: what he calls "*acquired character*" is "nothing other than the greatest possible familiarity with our own individuality."

[36] *The Captive*, III: 355; Kierkegaard, *Papers and Journals: A Selection*, 34 (*Papirer* I A 75; *KJN* AA: 12). On "the highest truth there is for someone *existing*," see Kierkegaard's pseudonymous *Concluding Unscientific Postscript*, trans. Alastair Hannay (Cambridge: Cambridge University Press, 2009), 171.

[37] Niklas Forsberg, *Language Lost and Found: On Iris Murdoch and the Limits of Philosophical Discourse* (New York: Bloomsbury, 2013), 185. See also Kant, *Critique of Judgment*, § 1.

[38] *The Fugitive*, III: 426.

[39] Joshua Landy, *How to Do Things with Fictions* (New York: Oxford University Press, 2012), 219n. On "extra-temporal being," see *Time Regained*, III: 904, and compare Landy, *The World According to Proust*, 84–86. With regard to what follows, in addition to this, see Ong, *The Art of Being*, 57.

[40] *Time Regained*, III: 913; see also *Within a Budding Grove*, I: 556–557.

apprehended is the self he was "always meant" or destined to be.[41] Unlike the conventional skeptic, who has no basis for anything besides going with the flow, he attains distinctiveness, the cardinal existential virtue. His truthfulness consists in his authenticity, and this authenticity is itself grounded in what he loves. As Scheler puts it, "the fullness, the gradations, the differentiations, and the power of [a person's] love circumscribe the fullness, the ... specificity, and the power of his possible spirit and of the possible *range* of contact with the universe," such that what this person loves—out of "all the being he can know"—is raised "out of the sea of [all] being like an island,"[42] defining the contours of his "individual destiny."

Thus, even once he has become "no more capable by an effort of memory of being still in love with Albertine than I was of continuing to mourn my grandmother's death," Marcel conceives of his literary art as a tribute to them, a posthumous "fulfillment" of what their lives have meant, just as his love for Gilberte had "unconsciously" prepared the way for his love of Albertine.[43] His life looks in retrospect to have been the story of how he has realized his vocation as an author, elevating in his written work his ordinary emotions into something at once based on them but also "more exalted, more pure, more true"—for without this elevation, "life would be meaningless."[44] His heart, made by his practice of loving and becoming concerned, bears the traces of who he is as a subject, as a spiritual being, and it situates him in a world that is too ambiguous, his feelings about it too ambivalent, to be completely embraced *or* rejected.

---

[41] On the notion of a divine vantage point that ratifies and sanctions one's destiny in this world, see Karl Britton, *Philosophy and the Meaning of Life* (Cambridge: Cambridge University Press, 1969), 192–193. For the conventional habits of the skeptic, see Jason Xenakis, "Noncommittal Philosophy," *Journal of Thought* 7 (1972): 199.

[42] Scheler, "Ordo Amoris," 106–111.

[43] *Time Regained*, III: 939–944; *The Captive*, III: 254.

[44] *The Captive*, III: 381; *Time Regained*, III: 935–936. Regarding the latter, see also Ricoeur, *Time and Narrative, Volume Two*, 131–134. On love and concern forming the heart, see Kierkegaard, *Works of Love*, 12. Finally, on ambiguity, see also Ong, *The Art of Being*, 226.

ii.

Nietzsche's term for a love that "would affirm luck, chance, and necessity," and "say yes to *everything* that exists," including "the whole chain of happenings that has led up to just the person that each of us is," is *amor fati*, the love of fate:[45] "I want to learn more and more how to see what is necessary in things as what is beautiful in them—thus I will be one of those who make things beautiful. *Amor fati:* let that be my love from now on!" Seeing *what is* as *what ought to be* qualifies, he tells us, as *creating* beauty. And nothing could pose so difficult a test for affirming life on such terms as suffering that "we do not want but which befalls us unbidden," the world as it happens to exist and as we have decidedly not willed it.[46] This is what challenges us to love what appears to be eminently not lovable. Of all the "infinite interpretations" that are available, collapsing "what ha[s] indeed taken place," for instance in the romance of Swann and Odette, into what seems "to have been inevitable,"[47] exemplifies the love of fate. And this is pertinent not only in those "hallowed moments" of the sort that have made it seem to the narrator "that life was worth living,"[48] but rather at all times.

The article of faith that *amor fati* involves is cast in what we might call the future perfect tense: namely, that everything which has transpired *will have made sense* in the end, if not from our standpoint, then from one that is in principle available. Kierkegaard writes that "it is quite true what philosophy says: that life must

---

[45] Simon May, *Love: A History* (New Haven, CT: Yale University Press, 2011), 189–196; Friedrich Nietzsche, *The Gay Science*, § 276.

[46] Béatrice Han-Pile, "Nietzsche and the Affirmation of Life," in *The Nietzschean Mind*, ed. Paul Katsafanas (London: Routledge, 2018), 448–467, 454. Cf. Nietzsche, *The Will to Power*, § 533, on the affirmation of "not only ourselves but all existence." See also *The Gay Science*, § 374, on the "*new 'infinite'*," made of "*infinite interpretations*." Cf. William James, *Psychology: The Briefer Course* (Notre Dame, IN: University of Notre Dame Press, 1985), 221: "Every reality has an infinity of aspects or properties."

[47] *Swann's Way*, I: 414.

[48] *Time Regained*, III: 1088. On "hallowed moments" that are felt as supremely meaningful, see James, *The Varieties of Religious Experience*, 347.

be understood backwards. But then one forgets the other principle: that it must be lived forwards," which means "that temporal life can never properly be understood" by one who exists in time and is thus always unfinished.[49] We pay for what Beckett calls "the sin of having been born" through our will to affirm all of life, by virtue of an "incurable optimism" which is associated with hoping that it ends up making sense somehow.[50]

Love of fate is predicated upon the belief that, if we wish for example to have a close and long-lasting friendship such as Marcel has with Robert de Saint-Loup, to celebrate the "felt truth" of a moment such as wishing that this kind and intelligent man "would take a liking to me, that I should be his best friend,"[51] and to rejoice in the developing friendship, then we must embrace, too, that Robert ends up frequenting male brothels, unhappily marrying Gilberte, and dying in the war "two days after his return to the front while covering the retreat of his men."[52] The "very special being" Robert "seemed to be" upon their first meeting, he "for whose friendship I had so greatly wished," *might* have survived longer, Marcel speculates—but didn't, and those who loved him must hereafter live with this. What "shocking disparities we should find," he muses, "if we did not take account of the future and the changes that it must bring, in a horoscope of our own riper years cast for us in our youth."[53]

"The universe is real for us all and dissimilar to each of us," every one of them "differing from all the rest as one universe differs from another," such that "we can truthfully say to other people, when speaking of these things of the past, that they can have no conception of them, that they are unlike anything they have seen,

---

[49] Kierkegaard, *Papers and Journals: A Selection*, 161 (*Papirer* IV A 164; JJ 167). Cf. Galen Strawson, *The Subject of Experience* (New York: Oxford University Press, 2017), 117.
[50] Beckett, *Proust*, 5 and 49.
[51] *Time Regained*, III: 926; *Within a Budding Grove*, I: 782–790.
[52] *Time Regained*, III: 877–878 and 884.
[53] *Within a Budding Grove*, I: 573.

and that we ourselves cannot inwardly contemplate without a certain emotion."[54] For "it is not one universe, but millions, as many as the number of human eyes and brains in existence, that awake every morning." It is no wonder, then, that our standpoints on the world do not compose a unity, as a universe corresponds to each; presenting "an infinite series of viewpoints," Proust's narrator "has the power to be the whole *of* these parts without totalizing them."[55] Each of them, as Marcel says, "expresses a genuine point of view," hence "one of the modes whereby the production of grief and pain is rendered possible." To grasp "that ineffable something which differentiates qualitatively what each of us has felt," a literary artist illustrates "the intimate composition of those worlds which we call individuals," providing us with the only true voyage, to see the universe through the eyes of another, of a hundred others, to see the hundred universes that each of them sees, that each of them is.[56]

We would not confuse our own way of seeing with anyone else's. However, even if I am Marcel I may glimpse what it is like to be some other person: perhaps Albertine in her bottomless desire, or perhaps my mother in what must be her even more acute emotions upon the death of Bathilde ("I realized with horror what she must be suffering," he says, by virtue of her greater closeness to Marcel's grandmother),[57] perhaps my grandmother herself who is dead ("how lonely she must be feeling"),[58] this woman to whom "all the genius that might have existed from the beginning of the world" would "have been less precious" than "a single one of my defects," so endlessly did she love me. Merleau-Ponty comments that love

---

[54] *The Captive*, III: 189–190; *Swann's Way*, I: 380; *The Captive*, III: 287; finally, again *The Captive*, III: 189–190. See also Merleau-Ponty, *Institution and Passivity*, 28: "As soon as [a love] is felt, it is true."

[55] Deleuze, *Proust and Signs*, 167–169.

[56] *The Captive*, III: 75 and III: 259–260. Cf. Britton, *Philosophy and the Meaning of Life*, 176.

[57] *Cities of the Plain*, II: 796.

[58] *Cities of the Plain*, II: 785–788. On the endurance of love and suffering, see Thiher, *Understanding Marcel Proust*, 227. See also *Cities of the Plain*, II: 787, on the "agonizing synthesis of survival and annihilation."

"allows us to see everything that someone is, how someone is the world itself," a world unto herself that is. And, "in exchange for what we imagined, life gives us something else," for it "results from ... circumstances chosen for other reasons," making us "discover not exactly what we were seeking, but something else."[59] To affirm joyfully whatever we are granted, we need the Kierkegaardian virtue of being jubilant: "the one whose joy is dependent on certain conditions is not joy itself," for his or her joy "is conditional."[60] True *amor fati*, by contrast, can only be unconditional.

It must embrace the fact that Albertine "was thrown by her horse against a tree while she was out riding," adding to Marcel's emotional reality something of which he had "never had any suspicion," precisely when what he needs above all is "her return."[61] One's sensibility, we are told, "receives, like the wake of a thunderbolt, the original and for long indelible imprint of the novel event," administering a "blow to the heart" that is "physical" in its force. In order, Marcel says, for news of the death of Albertine "to have been able to eliminate my suffering, the shock of the fall would have had to kill her not only in Touraine but in myself. There, she had never been more alive," as his grandmother remained alive in him many months after she had passed away in bodily form.[62] The truth of a loving subjectivity cannot be endorsed unless it accepts everything that is most deplorable to us, everything we would have wished to be otherwise.

---

[59] Merleau-Ponty, *Institution and Passivity*, 37–39.
[60] Kierkegaard, *Without Authority*, trans. Howard V. Hong and Edna H. Hong (Princeton, NJ: Princeton University Press, 1997), 37. Clément Rosset makes a similar point in *Joyful Cruelty*, trans. David F. Bell (Oxford: Oxford University Press, 1993), 15–17.
[61] *The Fugitive*, III: 485–486. What follows is from *The Fugitive*, III: 431. On "how feelings are affected by bodily states" in Proust, see Singer, *The Nature of Love, Volume Three*, 174.
[62] *The Fugitive*, III: 487; *Time Regained*, III: 950.

iii.

Marcel asks himself whether Albertine's death might actually have extended the duration of his love for her, and yet "this very question takes nothing away from the reality of what happened" between them.[63] What if, just once, we could live up to Nietzsche's noble formula of affirmation for a human being? We would clutch our concrete actuality as if it had been exactly what we wanted most of all, and would die holding onto what we have loved as the truth of our life, consenting to our facticity in spite of everything that gives us pause. "What we have to bring to light and make known to ourselves is our feelings, our passions, that is to say the passions and feelings of all mankind."[64] Proust's narrator adds that:

> a woman whom we need and who makes us suffer elicits from us a whole gamut of feelings far more profound and more vital than a man of genius who interests us. It is for us later to decide, according to the plane upon which we are living, whether an infidelity through which some woman has made us suffer is of little or great account beside the truths which it has revealed to us.

The truth of every human lifespan, apprehended through our emotions, is finally vindicated in Proust as the loftiest reality we can know: this is the perspective his fiction conveys. To perform this daunting task requires "courage of many kinds, including the courage of one's emotions," the "abrogation of one's dearest

---

[63] Merleau-Ponty, *Institution and Passivity*, 36. See also page 38: "What is not surpassed is the alterity of the other and finitude." What is given to us unchosen, by circumstances, may have been "secretly willed, not fortuitous," or so Proust indicates plainly. Regarding what follows, see Brian Treanor, *Melancholic Joy: On Life Worth Living* (New York: Bloomsbury Academic, 2021), 1–45 and 95–142.

[64] *Time Regained*, III: 944–945. See also *Within a Budding Grove*, I: 932, in which passage Marcel instructs us that "what we take, in the presence of the beloved object, is merely a negative, which we develop later, when we are back at home, and have once again found at our disposal that inner darkroom the entrance to which is barred to us so long as we are with other people."

illusions" and comforting lies and fabrications, for "it is only while we are suffering that we see certain things which at other times are hidden from us,"[65] namely, many difficult revelations about ourselves. As lost loves fade from our memory, we are no longer so disturbed by our grandmother's absence from this world, or by Gilberte's much smaller place in our life now. In terms of our life story, however, that we have loved these people, and that we have loved Albertine enough that she is unrivaled in our heart, leaves an imprint. It is part of what we will have become.

"I no longer loved Albertine. At most, on certain days, when the weather was of the sort which . . . by awakening one's sensibility, brings one back into relationship with the real, I felt painfully sad in thinking of her." He "was suffering from a love that no longer existed. Thus does an amputee, in certain kinds of weather, feel pain in the limb that he has lost."[66] This is the type of realization that we as readers are invited to hold like a magnifying glass up to our own experience, examining ourselves by means of À la recherche. The "book" that "has been dictated to us by reality" is the only one that "really belongs to us," through our impressions each of which "is for the writer what experiment is for the scientist."[67] "From ourselves comes only that which we drag forth from the obscurity . . . within us, that which to others is unknown."

> In reality every reader is, while he is reading, the reader of his own self. The writer's work is merely a kind of optical instrument which he offers to the reader to enable him to discern what, without this book, he would perhaps never have perceived.
>
> . . . In order to read with understanding many readers require to read in their own particular fashion, and the author must not be indignant at this; on the contrary, he must leave the reader

---

[65] *Time Regained*, III: 932–933.
[66] *The Fugitive*, III: 606.
[67] *Time Regained*, III: 913–914. Cf. Shattuck, *Proust's Binoculars*, 106.

all possible liberty, saying to him: "Look for yourself, and try whether you see best with this lens or with this other one."[68]

When unable to perceive significance in the world, he doubts the very possibility of meaning and thinks of "the materialist hypothesis, that of there being nothing" real.[69] Of Albertine, he declares that "I did not believe that she would have left the house without telling me, but my unconscious thought so."[70] We can have contradictory beliefs—we often do—and existence "laid bare and illuminated" is a question not of technique but of vision. "It is the revelation," Marcel attests, "of the qualitative difference, the uniqueness of the fashion in which the world appears to each one of us." Through "art alone are we able to emerge from ourselves" and share our felt sense of reality.[71] This, for Marcel, includes the manner in which he has sustained bonds with Albertine through his grief, since losing her. His literary work of art testifies to this.

iv.

This young woman, initially encountered in Balbec then later brought to Paris, whose entry into Marcel's life coincides with the arrival of spring and summer months, so that "I did not distinguish, in the pleasure that I felt, the return of Albertine from that of the fine weather,"[72] is a person for whom a world exists. And "to devote

---

[68] Proust, *Time Regained*, III: 949.

[69] *The Captive*, III: 388. The "moral of skepticism," as Cavell perceives, is "that the human creature's basis in the world as a whole . . . is not that of knowing, anyway not what we think of as knowing."—*The Claim of Reason*, 241.

[70] *The Captive*, III: 373.

[71] *Time Regained*, III: 931–932. On continuing bonds after death, see e.g., Kathleen Marie Higgins, "Love and Death," in *On Emotions: Philosophical Essays*, ed. John Deigh (Oxford: Oxford University Press, 2013), 159–178.

[72] *The Guermantes Way*, II: 364. See also Enns, "Love's Limit," 32: "No one can love . . . without this *wanting the other to be*." On loving either persons or inanimate objects, see Jollimore, *Love's Vision*, 22 and 26.

one's life to women" such as her is "more reasonable" than to dedicate it "to postage stamps or old snuff-boxes," collectible items that do not possess their own points of view or have their own worlds. Proust creates a framework for his narrator "that is outside Marcel's own aesthetic considerations,"[73] so we should not be astonished that his, that is Marcel's, theories do not include how the self revealed in love is never just identical to the self I already am but is a "self that I could possibly be or become," if I can remain "true to that revelation," as George Pattison avers,[74] the meaning of which "I can only speak of in fumbling, misleading, or, at any rate, inadequate terms." And, one might add, over thousands of pages of text. It is Marcel's conviction that the cohesion of his life depends on a series of loves: for his mother and grandmother, for Gilberte, for Robert de Saint-Loup, for the Duchesse de Guermantes, and finally for Albertine—not to mention *their* love for Marcel himself. Moreover, it "*feels* like" something to be convinced of this.[75]

"Enchantments of reality," in Beckett's terms, has the air of a paradox. But "when the object is perceived as particular and unique and not merely the member of a family, when it appears independent of any general notion ... then and then only may it be[come] a source of enchantment."[76] Skeptical doubt, by "awakening us to the temptation to transcend the human," ultimately "invites us to fall in love with the world," a world that may or not be *worth* our affective investment when analyzed in the dull light of cold reason. Love is therefore "what reveals the 'personality,'"[77]

---

[73] May, *Proust*, 69.

[74] George Pattison, *God and Being: An Enquiry* (New York: Oxford University Press, 2011), 231. Cf. Franck, *L'Écriture sensible: Proust et Merleau-Ponty*, 282–283.

[75] Landy, *How to Do Things with Fictions*, 127–128. See also Hadreas, *A Phenomenology of Love and Hate*, 20–21: "Husserl describes an 'I–You relation,'" one in which two striving subjects come to be related ... in mutual interactive affecting and being affected." Husserl uses the term "*aufeinander*" to capture this "understanding-following-after-another."

[76] Beckett, *Proust*, 11. The following quotation is from *The Human Embrace: The Love of Philosophy and the Philosophy of Love*, ed. Ronald L. Hall (University Park: Pennsylvania State University Press, 2000), 126. See also Cavell, *The Claim of Reason*, 431 and 477–496.

[77] Merleau-Ponty, *Institution and Passivity*, 37–38.

and "allows us to see everything that someone is, how someone is [a] world itself," that is, a world unto him- or herself. Our feelings both designate the properties of people and things *and*, in addition, "manifest, express, and reveal" the first person, "the inwardness of an I," at the same time.[78] Our loves, as well as the love of others for us, lend us a space in which to become what we are—that is, what we will have been.

Passionate understanding is the form of rationality that emerges out of this procedure, "an operation of the mind in which conviction" actually "creates the facts."[79] This is why existential truth requires the courage of one's emotions. As James and Kierkegaard would agree, "a rule of thinking" that would "prevent me from acknowledging certain kinds of truth if those kinds of truth were really there, would be an irrational rule."[80] We need the courage of our emotions to trust in the veracity of what love has disclosed.

"We always suppose an external universe," Hume says, even if we cannot prove that it exists; radical doubt, "were it ever possible to be attained by any human creature," would "be entirely incurable"[81]—displaying how belief is an act of the sensitive part of our nature, more than an acquiescence in the face of indubitable evidence. What turns out to be the true story of our lives depends on interpretation, which is always by its very nature subject to later reinterpretation.[82] The one who enacts this perceptual faith inhabits an enchanted world, one in which "a wine-merchant's girl at her cash-desk or a laundress chatting in the street" may seem like a veritable

---

[78] See Ricoeur, *Fallible Man*, 85.
[79] *The Captive*, III: 188. See also *Swann's Way*, I: 162.
[80] William James, "The Will to Believe," in *The Essential William James*, ed. Bruce W. Wilshire (Albany, NY: SUNY Press, 1984), 309–325, 325.
[81] David Hume, *An Enquiry Concerning Human Understanding*, 2nd ed., ed. Eric Steinberg (Indianapolis: Hackett Publishing Company, 1993), 103–104.
[82] Cf. Landy, *Philosophy as Fiction*, 115–122. See also Alexander Nehamas, "Nietzsche, Intention, Action," *European Journal of Philosophy* 26 (2018): 685–701, 693, using the example of an extra-marital affair to make the point that only in retrospect can we know what it has meant in our life story, either as a distraction or (perhaps) as the dawning of a new love that becomes foremost for us. On Marcel's sighting of, and writing about, the Martinville steeples, see *Swann's Way*, I: 196–198.

goddess.[83] And we perceive things this way only when we are emotionally affected. When Albertine was Marcel's prisoner, he did not appreciate her, because it seemed that her departure could be indefinitely postponed, like death. His love for her is at one stage merely "like an abstract truth, of no value until it had been tested by experience,"[84] but later it comes to be profoundly felt. How can we bear this sort of truth, and all the suffering that it causes us? New futures will forever continue to stretch ahead of us. Such is the character of possibility: there is perpetually more "subjective truth"[85] to dawn.

"I have always been more open to the world of potentiality than to the world of contingent reality. This helps one to understand the human heart, but one is apt to be taken in by individuals,"[86] Proust's narrator observes. *In Search of Lost Time* is largely the tale of how he has been "taken in" by particular contingent beings. The fact that our perception implicates our peculiar subjective orientation raises what Merleau-Ponty calls "the problem of a genuine *in-itself-for-us*." Although we cannot "conceive any perceived thing without someone to perceive it," and certainly no emotionally moving things without a subject who is moved, nevertheless "the thing presents itself to the person who perceives it as a thing in itself,"[87] and this is true of what we love. Albertine's existence, while she is alive, is quite independent of Marcel's mind and heart. Those whom he has loved, and the way he has loved them, define who he is, shaping the contours of his affective standpoint and his involvement with the world. Because, like any of us, Marcel is finite, he cannot respond to everything whatsoever—but he can strive to be true to what has moved him most deeply. He learns about his

---

[83] *The Captive*, III: 164. "Now that Olympus no longer exists," he suggests, "its inhabitants dwell upon the earth." See also *The Captive*, III: 167, at which point he claims that "the streets, the avenues are full of goddesses."

[84] Proust, *Cities of the Plain*, II: 1048. Cf. *Swann's Way*, I: 92; "the heart changes, and it is our worst sorrow."

[85] *The Captive*, III: 355; see Kierkegaard, *Concluding Unscientific Postscript*.

[86] *The Captive*, III: 16.

[87] Merleau-Ponty, *Phenomenology of Perception*, 375.

temperament and learns the truth about—not only *his* world, but *the* world—at the same time. Reality as we have felt it to be—as loving, emotional individuals—is the content of subjective truth. And this might be the highest truth that is attainable for an existing person.

Index

admiration 26, 35, 98
affirmation 21, 69, 98, 124, 128,
    131–2, 133–6, 137, 141
affordances 87–9
    see also possibilities
Agostinelli, Alfred 117
amazement 31
amor fati
    see affirmation
amusement 53
Anderson, R. Lanier 84–5
anger 52, 89
anguish
    see anxiety
anxiety x, 11, 64, 73–4, 92, 101, 113,
    123, 129
a priori, emotional 1–2, 5, 7, 68, 101
Aristotle 111
astonishment 33, 47, 108, 140
atmospheres, emotional 30, 71–2,
    86, 96–7
attunement
    see mood
awe 34, 36, 112

Baldwin, Thomas 71, 78n, 83n
Bales, Richard 78
Beattie, Ann 116
beauty 13–4, 17, 26, 28–30, 39, 46,
    48, 50, 54, 55, 67, 71–2, 78,
    85, 86, 97, 102, 118n, 124–
    6, 133; and *passim*
Beauvoir, Simone de 37n, 125
Beckett, Samuel 64, 97, 118, 126,
    134, 140
Bensussan, Gérard 102

Bersani, Leo 65n, 92n, 99, 107
bisexuality 49–50, 97, 107, 109–10,
    117, 128, 134
body
    see embodiment
boredom 101, 112–4
Bowie, Malcolm 40
Brée, Germaine 125–6
Brentano, Franz 81
Britton, Karl 131–2

Calhoun, Cheshire 18, 62
Camus, Albert 72–3
Carlisle, Clare 112
Carson, Anne 117
Cavell, Stanley 50, 103n, 113, 122,
    139n
chance
    see contingency
Colombetti, Giovanna 8, 36n, 88n,
    106n
contentment 52, 61, 92
contingency 16, 21–2, 26, 32, 54,
    62–4, 66, 69, 89, 92, 125,
    130, 137, 142
Cooper, David E. 82

death of a self 33, 53, 101
de Beistegui, Miguel 10n, 80
Deleuze, Gilles 7n, 36n, 78–9, 129,
    135
depression
    see melancholy
Descartes, René 75n, 108n
Descombes, Vincent 20, 51n, 54n,
    57n, 129

INDEX

de Sousa, Ronald 3, 37n
Deutsch, Eliot 106
Dewey, John 111, 114n
disdain 122
dismay 11, 16
disenchantment 33, 71
distinctiveness
  see particularity
Dylan, Bob xvi, 72

Eliot, T. S. 102
Ellis, Ralph 21
embarrassment 105–6
embodiment 6, 25, 29–32, 37–8, 50, 74–5, 88, 106, 120, 123
emotion
  see names of specific emotions
enchantment 9, 15, 29, 39, 51, 72, 125, 140–1
Enns, Diane 139
enthusiasm 29
euphoria 34
Evans, C. Stephen 103
exasperation 65
exhilaration 111–2
existential thought, contrasted with existentialism ix–x

Falck, Colin 46
fascination 27
fear 66, 97, 111–2, 135
Franck, Robert xii, 140
Frankfurt, Harry G. 7–8, 9n, 12n, 13, 20, 33n
Freud, Sigmund 7
Fuchs, Thomas 72n

Gautier-Vignal, Louis 77n
Gibson, James J. 88
Green, F. C. 68
grief 6–8, 38, 59, 87–9, 128, 132, 135–6, 138–9
Grimaldi, Nicolas 61n, 78n

Groarke, Leo 115, 119n
Gumbrecht, Hans U. 30

habit 111–4
Hägglund, Martin 128n
Hall, Ronald L. 140
Hamlet 33
Hankinson, R. J. 55
Han-Pile, Béatrice 133
happiness 29, 32, 96, 127
  see also beauty
Hare, R. M. 85
Heidegger, Martin x, 4n, 17, 35, 61, 83n, 88n, 103
Henry, Anne 73
Heraclitus 76
Herbert, George 116–7
Higgins, Kathleen M. 139n
Houston, John P. 46, 58
Hughes, Edward J. 45
Hume, David 141
Husserl, Edmund 9, 25n, 41, 73, 83, 96n, 126, 140

indifference 3–4, 7–8, 11–2, 20, 32, 51, 71–3, 76, 97–100, 102, 106
"infra-red" vision 2–4, 9, 12, 17, 23, 33, 37–8, 51, 107, 125
"in itself" 14, 17–9, 22, 24–5, 29, 31–2, 44–5, 57–8, 68, 73–4, 81, 90–4, 100, 106–7, 114, 116, 119, 123, 129, 142
introspection, rejection of term 59
inwardness, of the other
  see "in itself"

James, William 18, 43–4, 107, 122, 133, 141
Janaway, Christopher 105n
Jankélévitch, Vladimir 57
jealousy x, 11, 18, 61, 64, 66–7, 89, 92, 97, 98–9, 101, 107, 119–21, 123

INDEX

Jollimore, Troy 10n, 16, 20, 74n, 87, 117–8, 139
Jones, Peter 39, 65n
joy 21, 59, 69, 74n, 131, 136

Kagan, Jerome xiii
kaleidoscope 61, 131–2
Kant, Immanuel 6, 81, 85n, 95–6, 123
Kestenbaum, Victor 111, 114n
Kierkegaard, Søren ix–x, 2n, 7, 14, 16, 26, 49, 51–2, 59n, 64, 92, 103n, 112, 131, 133–4, 136, 141, 142–3
Krishek, Sharon 11n, 123n
Kristeva, Julia x, 77, 79, 130n
Krueger, Joel 88n, 106
Kubala, Robbie 40, 54n, 77n, 107
Kundera, Milan x, 46n, 119n

Ladenson, Elisabeth 110
Landy, Joshua 3n, 12, 20n, 27n, 48, 59, 62–3, 78n, 80, 92n, 95, 101, 108, 118, 128–9, 131, 140, 141
Large, Duncan 49
Leibniz, Gottfried W. 28
Lewis, David K. 27–8
Levinas, Emmanuel 31n, 37, 127n
Little, Margaret O. 36, 74n

Magee, Bryan 43
Mallarmé, Stéphane 117
Marion, Jean-Luc 10n, 17n
materialism 5–6, 63, 79, 83, 139
May, Derwent 108n, 126n, 140
May, Simon 133
meaning 2–4, 13, 17–8, 21, 32–3, 37, 51–4, 60, 63, 69, 72–3, 79, 83, 88, 94–5, 97, 99, 101, 103, 111, 119, 121, 125–6, 140
melancholy 36, 61, 97

Merleau-Ponty, Maurice 1, 14n, 28, 32n, 38n, 54, 55, 60, 67n, 76n, 77–8, 82, 89n, 104, 118n, 121, 128, 135–6, 137, 140, 142
Miller, J. Hillis 26
mood 30, 33–35, 38, 49, 56, 61, 66, 72, 77, 99
Mooney, Edward F. 11n, 82n
Moran, Richard 63
Mulhall, Stephen 34
Murdoch, Iris 15, 67, 98, 116, 118, 142–3

Nagel, Thomas 42, 58
narrative x–xi, 30, 82–3, 84n, 125, 131
Nehamas, Alexander 29, 40, 44, 67n, 80, 126, 127n, 141n
Nietzsche, Friedrich ix, xi, 13n, 36, 42, 47, 56, 64n, 69n, 77, 83n, 84, 96n, 99, 105–6, 114–5, 124, 133, 137
nihilism 17, 69, 72–3, 79
  see also materialism
nostalgia 36
Nussbaum, Martha C. 5, 6n, 40, 58, 64, 68n, 81–2, 103n, 113–4, 116–7, 123, 128

objectivity 14, 35, 51, 62, 119, 126
  see also indifference
Ong, Yi-Ping ix, 46n, 120
Ophelia 117
Ortega y Gasset, José 10–11, 15, 84n, 98, 122
other minds, problem of
  see "in itself"

partiality 12, 19, 22, 57, 84–5, 98, 123
particularity 9–10, 16, 20, 22, 33, 46, 48, 58–9, 61, 63, 65, 78, 100, 124, 129–32, 135, 139–41
Pattison, George 140

148 INDEX

perspective xii, 12, 16–7, 43–4, 49–50, 53, 56, 62, 66, 68–9, 83–5, 92, 93–4, 101–3, 105–6, 115, 119, 121–2, 124–7, 134–5, 137; and *passim*
pets 13, 42–5, 117
phenomenology x, 4, 8, 28–9, 33, 37, 59, 82–3, 101–2, 108, 140
  see also names of individual phenomenologists
Pippin, Robert 123, 127n
Plotinus 49
pluralism about truth xii, 84, 115, 130, 134–5
Popper, Karl 62
possessiveness 11, 22, 67, 80, 109–10, 119
possibilities 9, 11, 24–38, 61, 84, 88–9, 92, 105–6, 118, 140, 142
projection 5, 15–8, 33–4, 39, 46, 56–7, 66, 76–9, 81, 83, 95, 100, 108, 120–1
Proust, Marcel
  Author distinguished from narrator xi, 3, 49, 110
  Characters in *À la recherche du temps perdu*
    Albertine Simonet 3n, 4–5, 7–8, 12, 17–8, 20n, 21–2, 26–8, 30, 32, 39–40, 43–5, 47, 49–50, 53–6, 61–8, 70–8, 80–1, 86–7, 89–92, 94–7, 99–102, 104–9, 110, 112–4, 116–9, 121–2, 128–30, 132, 135–6, 137–40, 142
    as *pharmakon* 55
    eyes of 17, 31–2, 44, 66, 100, 105, 117, 122
    first appearance of, with friends 30–1, 44, 54, 66
    multiplicity of 91–2, 94, 117
    numerous known qualities of 107, 116–8

Andrée 14, 17, 63, 72, 74n, 75, 80n, 110, 128
Bergotte (author) 9
Bontemps, Madame 76
Charles Swann 12–6, 21, 45–6, 50, 53–4, 63, 70, 78, 80, 93, 98–9, 108, 119–21, 133
Charlus, Baron de 109–10
Elstir (painter) 48–9, 125, 126
fisher-girl, on bridge in Carqueville 25
Forcheville, Baron de 98–9, 120
Françoise 106, 113
Gilberte Swann 2–4, 9–10, 12, 21, 27, 33, 44, 51, 53, 62n, 76, 91, 102, 105, 132, 134, 138, 140
Gisèle 72
Golo 102
Grandmother of narrator (Bathilde) 6, 10, 29, 34, 52, 64n, 72, 79, 87–9, 99, 104-5, 122, 127–8, 130–2, 135–6, 138, 140
Guermantes, Duchesse de 91n, 120, 140
Guermantes, Duc de 118
Legrandin 70
Morel, Charlie 109
Odette de Crécy 12–6, 21, 45–6, 47–8, 53, 78, 80, 93, 98–9, 108, 118–21, 133
Parents of narrator 2, 26, 47–8, 54, 76, 122, 135, 140
Putbus, Madame, maid of 24
Rachel 19–21, 42–3, 47, 51, 83, 93
Rosamonde 72
Saint-Loup, Robert de 19–21, 28, 42–3, 47, 51, 90, 109, 134, 140
Stermaria, Mademoiselle de 24–5, 29, 67–8

Swann
  see Charles Swann
Uncle Adolphe 47–8
Verdurin, Madame 99n
Villeparisis, Madame de 29
Vinteuil (composer) 5n, 13–4, 57

rapture 35, 38
Ratcliffe, Matthew 3–4, 6n, 9n, 25, 33–4, 69
Rawlinson, Mary xii, 77
Reid, James D. 84, 111, 125n
relativism 50, 73, 95–9
Ricoeur, Paul x, 59, 60, 127, 141
Rilke, Rainer Maria xv, 84n, 88n, 119
Rivers, J. E. 75n
Roberts, Robert C. 5n, 34
Rorty, Richard 62, 124
Rosset, Clément 22n, 77n

Sachs, Marilyn M. 122n
sadness 4–5, 6, 8, 53, 69, 76, 138
Sartre, Jean-Paul 4, 11, 85, 94, 114, 120
Scheler, Max 1–2, 4, 12, 14, 16n, 19–20, 31n, 32–3, 50n, 82, 102–3, 106, 132
Schönbaumsfeld, Genia 123, 124n
Schopenhauer, Arthur 43, 58, 76n, 130–1
Sextus Empiricus xii, 40–115 *passim*
shame 22n, 121
Shattuck, Roger 61, 77n, 109n, 118
significance
  see meaning
Singer, Irving 86
solipsism 41, 73, 77n
Solomon, Robert C. 3, 102n
sorrow
  see sadness
Spinoza, Baruch 8, 17, 78
standpoint
  see perspective

Stoicism 68, 71, 73, 77–8
Stough, Charlotte L. 95
style, affective 60, 64, 67, 102–3, 126
  see also particularity, perspective
surprise 68, 100, 107, 112

temperament 61, 68, 85, 92n, 125–6, 129–30, 143
Thiher, Allen 108n, 120n
thing-in-itself
  see "in itself"
Thomson, Iain D. 83
Thoreau, Henry D. 32, 36n, 130n
Tietjen, Ruth R. 84
Tolstoy, Leo 122
Treanor, Brian 137

unconscious 60, 113n, 139
unknowable, the
  see "in itself"
unselfish love 9, 11, 15, 19–20, 64, 67–8, 79–80, 117, 123, 139

value
  see meaning
Vendrell Ferran, Íngrid 20n, 67n
von Hildebrand, Dietrich 119, 127n
vulnerability 6, 16, 21, 79, 113, 123

Warnock, Mary 82
Weil, Simone 67, 118n
Wilbur, Richard 1
Wimmers, Inge C. 12
Wittgenstein, Ludwig 41
Woodruff, Paul 57
worry 13–4, 62, 66, 95
Wynn, Mark R. 103

Xenakis, Jason 132n

Zahavi, Dan 34n, 106